Table of Contents

Chapter 1: Introduction - Who are the Cajuns and the Creoles

Chapter 2: Cajun and Creole Cuisine - What's in the Pot

Chapter 3: Seasoning the New Black Pot

Chapter 4: Breakfast

Chapter 5: Mardi Gras Eats

Chapter 6: Conclusion:

Master Chef reveals the secret recipes for many of America's favorite dishes. Now you can impress your family & friends with these unique recipes.

Be the first to have the recipes that everyone loves but nobody knows how to make including:

* KFC Original Recipe Chicken

* Boston Market Meatloaf

* Jack Daniel's BBQ Sauce

* Olive Garden Lasagna

* Junior's NY Cheesecake (As seen on TV)

* And over 200 more famous secret recipes!

Discover the ingredient combinations and spices

that make these foods taste so good.

Chapter 1: Introduction - Who are the Cajuns and the Creoles

For years when one hears the words "Cajun" and "Creole" it makes one think of New Orleans, Marie Laveau, Congo Square and Jazz. In truth these are two side by side cultures of two distinct groups of people who parallel in many regards in one region of the Good Old US of A. They are two ethnic groups of people residing in the same region of Louisiana, one of the Southern States in the United States of America.

When we think of Creole we think of mixed bi racial people that have descended from forefathers in New Orleans and Louisiana. This is partially true but it isn't the whole definition of what a person of Creole heritage is. In reality the Creole's were the first Europeans that settled in New Orleans and in the Mississippi Plantation Regions. Those original creoles considered themselves of aristocratic ancestry and were wealthy many times. They were descendents of French, Spanish and Portuguese Europeans who located in those regions.

The word itself "Creole" derives from the "Latin" word "creare" meaning to beget or create. After what was considered the "New World's" discovery; Portuguese colonists (slave traders) used the word "crioulo" to denote a slave of African Descent that was born in the "New World". After that for a time the world Creole was the designated word to describe all the New World colonists regardless of ethnic origin living along the Gulf Coast in particular Louisiana.

There the Spanish introduced the word "criollo" during Louisiana's colonial period from 1699 to 1803. Eventually the word's connotation grew to mean anyone of African or European heritage in that area. By the middle of the 19th century the word Creole implied those Black, White and Mixed persons who were not of Anglo Saxon heritage or foreign born Anglo Saxons. Creoles of Color (or gens de "couleur libre", "free persons of color") became their own ethnic group. Being half white they enjoyed many of the legal rights and privileges of white people.

They occupied a middle ground between the black slaves and whites. Many of the Creoles of Color owned property and had formal educations. Some were given high political appointments by the crown. Creole holdings involved shipping, banking and plantation ownership. Their businesses faltered after the Civil War without slave labor. However after the Civil War, the majority lost their status and joined the ranks of the impoverished black former slaves. The word "Creole" did sustain itself as a term also to white upper class Louisianans of non Cajun origin. This was confusing at times because Cajuns were called Creoles by people who were outsiders not indigenous to the region. This was mainly due to the fact that those outside of Louisiana were not familiar with the various differences of the ethnic groups there. Just like the Creoles of Color the White Creoles (called French Creoles) also suffered socio-economic decline after the Civil War.

In Arcadiana which was the part of French Speaking Louisiana where the Cajuns resided the newly impoverished Creoles married lower class Cajuns and assimilated into the Cajun culture. Today the word Creole is mainly used in Arcadiana to describe those of full or mixed African American Heritage. It is still understood that the term "Creole of Color" means creoles of mixed race heritage.

Black Creole means those who are predominately African American that are not mixed. In the past there was animosity between the two African descent groups based on color and social standing but today both are concerned with preserving the Creole culture together.

The term Creole still has vast grey areas where black, white and mixed race people may claim exclusivity to being the true Creole ethnically in relation to others who consider themselves Creole also.

Arcadians/Cajuns who originated from the West Coast of France primarily Brittany and Normandy first settled in Nova Scotia in 1604. They were for the most part peasants with little or no education at all and worked with their hands as a result. They were loaded on ships by the British after being expelled from Nova Scotia and began arriving in Louisiana in 1705. The Cajuns settled in the Bayous and open prairies. There they fished, farmed and traded what they trapped.

The Cajuns who were descendants of French Speaking Arcadians lived in isolation since their eviction from Nova Scotia in the early 1700 until modern times. It wasn't until the Oil Boom came that they had to fight to survive. So they hunted fished and gathered what they could selling the best to the outsiders and lived off of the leftovers. This is also what inspired Cajun cooking; which like Slave Food derived from the scrapes left over from the Plantation big house. In essence Cajun Food was anything that was edible that was not sold that could still be eaten. Cajun cuisine became a combination of making meals out of left overs and overlapping with the flavors of the south in addition to its Arcadian Roots.

"Arcadiana" also known as Cajun country spreads over a large area from the swamps in the bayous right up to the outskirts of New Orleans. They say the most interesting and robust Cajun food comes from Opelousas, Henderson, Breaux Bridge and Ville Platte - all small towns in south Louisiana. As you move down the swampy wet lands of the Atchafalaya Basin and its bayous which is the land of crawfish; the food gets milder but less delicious. Although Cajun food tastes good it doesn't necessarily look good. It's basically hearty country peasant food. Much of it is one pot food or food in pots such as stew type food. The pretty food that is in restaurants that is listed as Cajun goes against the grain of Cajun food traditionalists.

In terms of cooking; in broader terms Creole cuisine is "City" cooking based on French Traditions but influenced by the Spanish,

African and the other ethnic groups that make up Creole nationalities. Cajun food is considered "Peasant" food that the Arcadians traditionally later evolving into Cajun. Cajun cuisine developed as they learned to live in the swamps of Southern Louisiana. By nature creole food is more refined and subtler while Cajun food is more spicy and pungent.

One of the main factors that makes the two types of food distinct is the fact that both groups took different paths once they got here in the new world. Cajuns isolated themselves in swamp areas and remained as such while Creoles were integrated into cosmopolitan life. The french quarters in New Orleans became the Creole Sector. What happened is many other Americans began to come to New Orleans to build their homes and businesses and Canal Street which was the main dividing line was the thoroughfare for the Creole French Quarters and the rest of the City and its inhabitants. So Creole food became cosmopolitan and blended with the many cultures that settled in New Orleans. This lent a certain sophistication to Creole cuisine that the Cajun cuisine did not have.

In 1880 writer George Washington Cable made an observation about the distinction of Creole Cuisine in his book "Old Creole Days. His book was so popular that it made Creole culture and Cuisine a popularity. A few years later at New Orleans first World's Fair called "The Cotton Centennial" Cable who collaborated with Lafcadio Hearn. They wrote the first guidebook to New Orleans. Included in the book was descriptions of foods that were recognizable. They also pointed out that the food from New Orleans was different from anywhere else.

As the two cultures kept intertwining there has been a love of evolution of the two cooking styles as well. Today you will find some inland Cajun dishes different in some regards to the ones from the Bayou Cajun dishes as they are different from the Creole food served in New Orleans. In actuality a lot of the distinction has also been lost because the two cultures are so intermingled. In truth both Cajun and Creole food in terms of seasonings are more alike than dissimilar. What happens is you find subtle differences as you go from area to area in the region and that's what makes the two styles different. There are however dishes that are distinctly Cajun and Creole.

What you can say is there are similarities and differences between Cajun and Creole cooking. The Cajuns base a large portion of their Cuisine on stews, gumbos, okras and rice dishes. Creole food incorporates European food and African traces into its repertoire. If you were to compare a Cajun Jambalaya to a Creole Jambalaya the first thing you would notice is the color. Cajun Jambalaya is Brown while Creole Jambalaya is Red because of the tomatoes in it. Gumbo has a smokier flavor as you move out of New Orleans and into Cajun country. Both cooking style uses a roux to thicken the Gumbo. Creole food is more tomato based while Cajun roux based. The major differences in seasonings has merged for the most part. Both use rice, flour and oil for roux, crab, shrimp, oysters, crawfish, fish, frog, turtle, pork, beans, tomatoes, okra, yams, and pecans. Seasonings used by both cuisines are: parsley flakes, onion powder, garlic powder, salt, cayenne pepper, black pepper, and white pepper.

Chapter 2: Cajun and Creole Cuisine - What's in the Pot

So we established that Cajun people are the French Speaking Arcadians that were immigrants from Arcadia in Canada that the British kick out of Canada, Nova Scotia. They ended up in Arcadiana region of Louisiana USA. Cajun food is considered rustic food. It is made of local ingredients with simple preparations.

Creole people on the other hand; were those who are originally from French, Spanish and Portuguese Europeans first that mixed other ethnic descendants who landed in Louisiana. They mixed with the different cultural groups including Cajuns which gives their cuisine a distinct flavor as well. According to Chef John Folse creole cooking blends the distinct ethnic components of Louisiana into one flavor. Some of the contributions are still alive and well in the dishes eaten today in this region. Gumbo which is a Louisiana favorite tradition originally began from the French soup Bouillabaisse. The Spanish contributed spices and the dish Paella which became Jambalaya. The Germans brought cattle to the region namely pigs and chicken. It was the Native American Indians who introduced corn to the settlers as well as ingredients like sassafras and bay leaves. The Africans contributed "kin gumbo" okra. Each ethnic group brought something to the new land that went into the pot. Creole cooking also relies heavily on milk, butter and sausage all the remainders of French Cuisine.

Authentic Cajun Meals usually consist of three pots. One pot is dedicated to the main dish, one to steamed rice, skillet corn bread or some other grain dish and the third is whatever vegetable is around in bounty. Both Cajun and Creole cooking use what is called the holy trinity. These are the three aromatic staple seasoning vegetables; namely bell peppers, onions and celery. The three are finely diced and combined in cooking in a method similar to mire "poix" in traditional french cuisine. "Mire Poix" in french cooking combines finely diced onion, celery and carrot instead. In Creole and Cajun cooking the bell pepper replaced the carrot. Characteristic seasonings in Cajun and Creole cooking are parsley, bay leaf, green onions or scallions and dried cayenne pepper.

The Arcadian refugees that came from Nova Scotia and New Brunswick adapted their French rustic cuisine to the local ingredients that were available. Local ingredients include rice, crawfish, sugar cane and sassafras. Cajun cooking relied heavily on game which was supplemented with rice or corn. Cajun cooking also has hints of quite naturally French with Spanish and even some native American in it. Another feature of Cajun cuisine is the use of smoked meats. This is another common aspect of Cajun cooking.

Creole cooking is thought of to be more aristocratic or continental than Cajun cuisine. Creole cuisine uses a lot of the ingredients that was brought to this part of the world in addition to the local ingredients. Both cuisines do however make use of what is on hand at the time and incorporate local ingredients to the basic foods in their dishes.

Some of the Cooking techniques used in Cajun and Creoles use cuisine are:

1. Barbecuing- slow to low cooking technique like "Texas Cuisine" But with Cajun Seasonings; can involve grilling or baking.

2. Grilling- direct heat on a shallow surface; fastest of the different varieties of grilling which also include: Charbroiling which is direct dry heat on a solid surface with wide raised ridges; Gridironing which is direct dry heat on a solid or hollow surface with narrow raised ridges Griddling-direct dry or moist heat along with the use of oils or butter on a flat surface

3. Braising- combining a direct dry heat charbroil-grill or gridiron-grill with a pot filled with broth for direct moist heat, faster than smoking but slower than regular grilling or baking; time starts fast then slows down then speeds up again to finish.

4. Baking- direct and indirect dry heat in an oven or furnace; faster than smoking but slower than grilling

5. Boiling- As in boiling crabs, crawfish or ship in seasoned liquid

6. Deep Frying

7. Etoufféé- cooking a vegetable or meat in its own juices, similar to braising but in New Orleans they call this "smothering" (Southern cuisine uses "smothering" also with a gravy)

8. Frying-also known as pan frying

9. Injecting-Using a large cooking syringe to infuse seasonings deep inside of meats through incisions made in them. This is a newer technique but is used all

across Cajun Country.

10. Stewing -also called "fricassee"

Cajuns also deep fry turkey or oven roast Turduckens (which are combinations of deboned Turkeys with deboned ducks inside of them and debone chickens inside the duck.) So turduckens have all three birds one inside the other. This is a more recent addition to Cajun cuisine as is blackened fish or chicken and also barbecuing shrimp in the shell. All these are not traditional Cajun cooking.

The main staple grains used in Cajun and Creole Cuisine are:

1. Corn

2. Rice-long, medium and short white rice grains are all used as is popcorn rice. In early Arcadia rice was considered a valuable item. Because the climate was conducive it was grown all over the region even wild. Rice became the predominant starch because it was easy to grow, store and prepare. The oldest rice mill in the United States is the Conrad Rice Mill In Iberia Louisiana.

3. Wheat-is used for baking mainly breads- They do use Flour meals and grains as well. White flour, corn flour and corn meal are common flour used.

The main staple fruits and vegetables depending on what's in season are:

1. Bell Peppers

2. Black Berries

3. Cayenne Peppers

4. Celery

5. Cucumbers

6. Figs

7. Limes

8. Lemons

9. Mirlitons also called Chayotes or Vegetable Pears

10. Muscadines

11. Okra

12. Onion

13. Pecans

14. Satsuma Oranges

15. Scallions(also known as green onions)

16. Squash

17. Strawberries

18. Sweet Potatoes

19. Tabasco Pepper

20. Tomatoes (mainly in Creole Cuisine)

21. Beans (canned and Fresh) Red Beans and Black Eyed Peas are a must

22. Chili peppers

Cajun folks had to learn how to preserve meats because of lack of refrigeration in the past. Smoking meats still occur today but such preparations as a turkey or duck confit (which was a turkey or duck preserved in poultry fat with spices is seen as quaint and almost nonexistent now. Hunting game is still wide spread in Arcadiana. Also the increase of Cat Fish farms along the Mississippi Delta has brought an increase of using it in cooking where before traditionally wild caught trout was used. The wild trout was the salt water species and red fish.

Both Cajuns and Creoles use quite a lot of Seafood.

Here is a List of some of the main ones used in Cajun Cuisine: Both use Crab, Shrimp and Oysters as well as the Crawfish

1. Bass
2. Catfish
3. Trout
4. Sac-au-Lait (White Perch or Crappie)
5. Yellow Perch

Saltwater or Brackish Water Species

1. Trout
2. Red Fish
3. Pompano
4. Drumfish
5. Flounder
6. Grouper
7. Perch-many varieties
8. Snapper

Shell Fish

1. Crawfish-Either Wild Swamp or Farm Raised
2. Shrimp
3. Oysters

4. Blue Crab

Also as part of the Sea Food Mix are what are called "Trash Fish". Trash fish are those fish that don't sell in the fish market because of their high bone to meat ratio or that they are complicated to cook. These are the type of fish the fishermen brought home to feed their families with. Examples are Garfish, Black drum also called Gaspergou or just "Goo", Croaker, and Bream.

Poultry

Farm Raised

1. Turkey (and Turkey Confit)

2. Chicken (and Guinea Hen)

Game Birds

1. Dove

2. Goose

3. Quail

4. Duck (and Duck Confit)

Pork

1. Andouille-   A spicy dry smoked sausage; characterized by a course ground texture

2. Boudin -   A fresh sausage made with green onions, pork and rice. Pigs blood is sometimes used to make "Boudin Rouge"

3. Chaurice- Similar to Spanish Chorizo

4. Chaudin-A pigs stomach stuffed with spiced pork and smoked. Also known as

"Pounce"

5. Ham Hocks-Is the joint between tibia and fibula and the metatarsals of the foot of a pig; where the foot is attached to the hog's leg.

6. Head Cheese- Is a cold cut that originated in Europe. Another version is pickled with vinegar and known as "Souse." It is not cheese at all but rather a meat jelly made from the flesh of the head of either a calf, cow, pig or sheep in aspic.

7. Gratons- Hog cracklings or pork rinds. Gratons are seasoned, fried pork skin and fat with occasional pieces of meat attached. Similar to Spanish Chicarrones

8. Fresh Pork Sausage- Neither smoked or cured; but highly seasoned. Mostly used in Gumbos. This sausage does not have rice in it which is what makes it different from Boudin

9. Tasso-a highly seasoned pork shoulder

Beef and Dairy

Beef isn't a main meat in Cajun or Creole cooking. But dairy products are used in the desserts and some of the bread and breakfast foods.

Other meats include:

1. Alligator

2. Frog Legs

3. Gros Bec commonly called Night Heron

4. Nutria or Coypu (a semiaquatic rodent)

5. Rabbit

6. Turtle (farm raised)

Herbs, spices and the use of seasonings play an important role in Cajun and Creole cooking.

Individual Seasonings

1. Bay Leaf

2. Oregano

3. Bell Peppers (Red or Green)

4. Black Pepper

5. Cayenne Pepper

6. Celery

7. Garlic

8. Onion

9. Parsley(Flat Leaf)

10. Sassafras Leaves dried and ground into a spice known as file(accent over the e) for gumbo

11. Sugar Cane; also cane syrup, brown sugar and molasses

12. Thyme

13. Holy Trinity- Onion, Celery and Bell Pepper

14. Allspice

15. Cinnamon

16. Cloves

17. Dill Seed

18. Mustard Seed

19. Peppercorns

20. Salt

Blended Seasonings

1. Hot Sauce

2. Seafood Boil Mix

3. Vinegar seasoned with small hot green pickled peppers is a common condiment with Cajun and Creole meals

4. Persillade-a sauce or seasoning mixture of parsley (French: persil) chopped together with seasonings including garlic, herbs, oil, and vinegar.

5. Marinades made with olive oil, brown sugar and citrus juices

6. Various barbecue rubs similar to other states

Whole peppers are rarely used in Cajun cooking. Ground Cayenne, Paprika and Pepper Sauces predominate.

Oils

1. Butter

2. Bacon Fat

3. Lard(pork grease)

4. Peanut oil

5. Vegetable oil

6. Olive oil

Bases

Cajun and Creole Cuisine uses different bases in their cooking style. The Cajuns and the Creoles inherited Roux from the French.

Roux- Is made with oil or bacon fat mixed with flour, which is used as a thickening agent especially in Gumbo and Etouffée It is made with equal parts of flour and fat.

Stocks- Are seasoned liquids used as bases for soups, stews, braising, poaching and other things. Cajun Stocks are more heavily seasoned than those in Continental cooking. Unique to Cajun cooking are shell fish stocks with the heads of crawfish and shrimps.

Type of Stocks

Fish or Court Bullion

Shellfish Stock

Chicken Stock

These are just some of the main things used in the Art of Cajun and Creole Cuisine.

Chapter 3: Seasoning the New Black Pot

Most Cajun and Creole people have Black Cast Iron Pots (or frying Pans) that have been passed down from generation to generation. This is the coveted cookware. Nothing makes the food taste better than one of these broken in pots. One of the reasons they cook so well and the food has such a good taste is because the pot is what is called "Seasoned". Seasoning is a process you do before you use a new pot. What happens when you season a pot is the pores in the pot (which is cast iron for those traditional cooks) absorbs the oil creating a natural non stick surface. The more the pot or pan is used the more seasoned it becomes.

The first thing you do if you just bought a new cast iron cookware such as a pot, dutch oven or frying pan; is to wash, rinse and dry the new pot thoroughly. If you also bought utensils it is recommended to wash them and then dry them over a low flame for two to three minutes. It removes all the moisture from the metal which is porous.

For the utensils; you then put two tablespoons of a liquid vegetable oil on the utensil. Do Not use a saturated fat such as butter or bacon fat because it will turn rancid on the utensil when you store it. Use a paper towel to completely coat the entire surface of the utensil. Including corners edges and if it has a lid that too. Do the same for the pot.

Next preheat the oven to 500 degrees F for 30 minutes. Line a large cookie sheet or baking pan with aluminum foil. Place the utensils on the sheet and the pot on the sheet upside down. Also place the lid on the sheet right side up. Bake the utensils for one hour. Turn off the heat and keep the pot in the oven for the next 4 to 6 hours with the door closed cooling down. Remove the pot and wipe down with a paper towel. This completes the seasoning process.

General Care of Your Seasoned Pot

Always wash with a mild detergent and make sure to rinse and then dry completely. Dry the utensils over heat for 2 to 3 minutes like the original seasoning process. Never put the pot or utensils in a dishwasher or scour with a metal or hard abrasive. You may use a plastic mesh pot cleaner bun to get those burnt spots off.

For the first few times using your new pot cook your food with very little water content. Also avoid those foods with a high acidic content such as tomatoes unless combined with other foods. Remove the lid off the pot when you take it off the heat because if you leave it on to steam it can remove the seasoning you did. If for any reason you taste rust or a metallic taste the pot is not adequately seasoned and you need to repeat the process.

Keep in mind cast iron cook ware heat evenly so it is not necessary to have a very high flame. The best cooking results are gotten on a medium to medium high temperature setting. Do not over heat or leave empty pots or utensils on the burners. Likewise do not place utensils on a hot burner. Allow pots or utensils to heat as a burner does.

When you store your cast iron cookware always leave the lids off so moisture doesn't collect. Store in a warm dry place. The black finish that cooks covet develops over time with steady use. You just created a family heirloom to pass on.

Caring for An Old Black Cast Ware Pot

As you use these type of cooking ware over the years they develop a crust that no amount of cleaning will remove. To clean an old pot here are the steps:

1. Wash the pot as normal

2. Place the washed pot in an open fire, a fire place, wood heater or campfire.

3. Allow pot to cook until residue is removed.

4. HANDLE WITH CARE ITS HOT....when the residue is sufficiently cleaned remove from the fire and set aside allowing the pot to cool slowly until it is cool enough to hold.

5. Use moist sand and a cloth to clean the pot both inside and out.

6. Re season as you would a new pot.

Chapter 4: Breakfast

Bon matin, et bon appetit! Good Morning and Good Eating!!!

Here are some typical recipes you would find in a Creole or Cajun home in the morning. It's not uncommon to find the nights left overs next to an egg in Bayou country. In New Orleans Creole breakfasts include fancy egg dishes to a good old french doughnut called a beignet. Cajun cooking is about big black cast iron cooking. New Orleans uses the cast iron pots but the presentation is more refined.

Both Cajun and Creole Cuisine have versions of French toast. Pan Perdu or Lost Bread is what its called. Here is both a Cajun and Creole recipe. The name came about Pain Perdue as a solution to bread that was about to be "lost" or thrown away because it was stale. Keep in Mind the french word for bread is Pan.

Pain Perdu Cajun Style

Traditionally any leftover or stale bread was used to make this recipe. It is not recommended however to use sourdough bread. Especially for the Variation recipe.

Ingredients

1 egg

2 tablespoons Sugar

1 Cup Milk

Dash of Nutmeg

2 Tablespoons Butter

Preparation:

Beat the Eggs and Sugar together add in Nutmeg and Milk, Dip slices of bread in the Egg/Milk mixture. Fry in the hot butter until brown on both sides. Dust with powdered sugar and then top with your favorite syrup. (Traditionally cane syrup or molasses was used. In addition to any local fruit or jelly that was preserved from a local fruit.)

Pan Perdue Creole Style

Stale french bread was the preferred bread for this recipe. This is not your typical french toast recipe. Its New Orleans Style french toast made using thin slices of french bread soaked in a custard like batter and then lightly or golden fried.

Ingredients

2 eggs

1/2 cup of milk

pinch of salt

1 tsp sugar

1 tsp vanilla

1/2 teaspoon cinnamon

1/4 tsp all spice

6 thick slices of day old french bread (older is finer as long as you can cut it and italian bread works fine too, in fact any crusty bread will work.)

1 tablespoon vegetable oil

powdered sugar (optional)

Preparing the Custard: Its the simple milk and egg custard that's the secret that makes Pain Perdue special. In a large mixing bowl whisk together your eggs, milk, salt, sugar, vanilla, cinnamon, and allspice.

Slicing the Bread:

Slice the bread into thick slices, at least 1-inch thick and add to the egg mixture. I used a beautiful whole-grain French loaf, but any French or Italian loaf should work nicely. Slicing at a slight angle will make for a longer piece of bread.

Soaking the Bread in the Custard:

Toss the slices until all the mixture has been absorbed into the bread. Depending on how stale the bread is this may take from 5 to 10 minutes. The secret to this recipe is to completely saturate the bread. This is also why thick slices of stale bread is used as thinner fresh bread would fall apart.

Lightly Browning the Bread Before Baking

Preheat oven to 400 degrees F.

In a large non-stick skillet, over medium heat, very lightly brown the slices in the butter and oil for about 2 minutes per side. Don't cook too dark as most of the browning will occur in the oven as the

French Toast Bakes.

Putting French Toast in Hot Oven:

Transfer to a baking sheet and bake at 400 degrees F. for 10 minutes.

Turning Over the Slices and Finishing the Baking

After 10 minutes remove, turn over and put back in the oven for another 5 minutes to brown the other side.

After 10 minutes on one side and 5 on the other the custard should be cooked on the inside, and the French toast will be crisp on the outside. If it looks like it needs more time cook it longer, but be careful not to cooked very dark as the egg custard may become bitter.

Serve Hot with Syrup and/or Fruit Sauces ...Hey, Where's the Powdered Sugar?

Traditionally it was served with powdered sugar but You can add syrup and or fruit sauces.

A variation on this recipe would be to use:

8 stale slices of french bread

1 cup half and half as opposed to 1 cup whole milk

4 beaten large eggs

1/4 cup of either sugar or simple syrup

2 teaspoons of Vanilla extract

A few gratings of fresh nutmeg

4 tablespoons butter

2 tablespoons powdered sugar mixed with 1/2 teaspoon cinnamon

In this version you let the oil and butter sizzle in a skillet before you add the soaked bread slices.

In this recipe the custard consists of the half-and-half or milk, eggs, sugar, vanilla and nutmeg and mix thoroughly in a large bowl. Like the previous recipe; soak the bread until the custard is completely absorbed. Meanwhile, melt the butter in a heavy skillet and add the oil.

When the butter and oil mixture is very hot, fry the soaked bread slices one or two at a time on each side, until golden brown. Drain on paper towels and hold in a warm oven until all the slices are cooked. Keep the fried slices warm in a 200 degree F oven while you finish cooking the rest.

To serve, Sprinkle with cinnamon and powdered sugar mixture just before serving. Serve with Louisiana cane syrup (cane syrup) , a strongly-flavored honey or any good syrup of your choice (real maple or fruit syrups are lovely too, but avoid that artificially-flavored pancake syrup).

This recipe serves 4.

The last version of this Recipe by Chef John Folse is Crème Brûlée Lost Bread. This is the most unique one out of the recipes I found

Prep time: 1 1/2 hours

Serves: 6

Ingredients:

12 French bread croutons, cut 1-inch thick

1/2 cup melted butter

1 cup brown sugar, lightly packed

2 tbsp's honey

5 eggs

1 cup milk

1/2 cup heavy whipping cream

1/8 tsp cinnamon

1/8 tsp nutmeg

1 tbsp vanilla

1 tbsp praline liqueur or Frangelico

Preparation:

French bread croutons should be cut out of a baguette-style loaf. These slices should be approximately 2 1/2 - 3 inches in diameter and 1 inch thick.

In a cast iron skillet, combine butter, brown sugar and honey over medium-high heat. Cook mixture, stirring constantly, until bubbly and sugar has dissolved.

Pour Brûlée into the bottom of a 13" x 19" x 2" baking dish. Allow Brûlée to cool slightly then top with the French bread croutons.

In a large mixing bowl, whisk eggs, milk, whipping cream, cinnamon, nutmeg, vanilla and liqueur. Blend thoroughly the pour evenly over the croutons.

Using the tips of your fingers, press bread down gently to force the custard into the croutons without breaking. Cover dish with clear wrap and chill overnight.

Preheat oven to 350 degrees F. Allow custard to sit out at room temperature, approximately 1 hour. Bake, uncovered, until French toast is puffed and edges of the croutons are golden brown, approximately 40 minutes. Allow to cool 10 minutes prior to serving.

When ready to serve, remove 2 of the Lost Bread Croutons per guest and invert them onto the center of a 10-inch plate. Top with powdered sugar and drizzle lightly with honey.

Another " Breakfast Distinction" between the two Cuisines is the Difference between the bread puddings served by Creole Kitchens and that of a Cajun. Creole bread pudding that is eating for breakfast is sweet like a desert bread pudding while Cajun breakfast bread pudding is not its a hardy meal. For a creole breakfast a scoop of Bread pudding topped with a Burbon whiskey sauce would start the meal going.   While a Cajun bread pudding is a big part of the hearty meal.

Cajun Breakfast Bread Pudding:

This recipe serves 6

Ingredients

1 tablespoon butter for greasing baking dish

olive oil for sautéing

1 cup yellow onions, roughly chopped

1/2 cup green bell peppers, roughly chopped

1/2 cup red bell peppers roughly chopped

1/2 teaspoon sea salt

1/4 teaspoon freshly ground black pepper

2 cloves minced garlic

1 tablespoon fresh Italian parsley leaves, minced plus more for garnish

3 links Andouille or Louisiana sausage, chopped

6 large eggs

2 cups whole milk

1/2 cup heavy cream

1-3/4 teaspoons Cajun Seasoning

6 cups day old French or Italian bread*

8 ounces grated Fontina or smoky Gouda cheese (about 2 cups)

1/2 cup fine dry bread crumbs

1/2 cup freshly grated Parmesan

2 tablespoons melted butter

If baking right away, preheat the oven to 350°F. Lightly grease a 9 by 13-inch baking dish with 1 tablespoon butter and set aside.

Add 2 - 3 teaspoons olive oil to a medium skillet. Heat over medium high heat until the oil is hot but not smoking. Add the onions, bell peppers, 1/4 teaspoon of the salt, and 1/8 teaspoon of the pepper and cook, stirring, until soft, 3 minutes. Add the garlic and cook, stirring, for about 1 minute. Stir in the parsley, cook for another minute, and then remove from the heat. Transfer to a bowl or plate and allow to the vegetables to cool.

Heat the skillet (you can reuse the vegetable skillet) over medium high heat. Add 1-2 teaspoons olive oil. Add the sausage to the skillet and cook, stirring, until lightly browned, 5 to 6 minutes. Drain the sausage on paper towels and allow to cool.

In a large bowl, beat the eggs. Add the milk, cream, 1 teaspoon of Cajun seasoning and the remaining 1/4 teaspoon salt and 1/8 teaspoon pepper. Whisk to combine.

Fold in the bread cubes and let sit for 15 minutes. Add the cooked sausage, the onion mixture, and the Fontina (or Gouda) cheese. Stir gently to combine all of the ingredients. Pour into the prepared baking dish, cover with aluminum foil.

At this point, you can bake the bread pudding in the preheated oven until the center is just set, about 50 to 55 minutes or you can refrigerate for up to 1 day and then bake. Remove from the refrigerator 30 minutes before baking.

Meanwhile, combine the bread crumbs, Parmesan, melted butter, and remaining 3/4 teaspoons Cajun seasoning. Uncover the bread pudding and sprinkle the bread crumb mixture evenly over the top. Return to the oven, increase the heat to 375 degrees F and bake uncovered until the bread pudding is completely set in the center, puffed, and golden brown on top, about 20 minutes. Garnish with a few tablespoons minced parsley.

Allow to sit for 15 minutes before serving.

Creole Bread Pudding : This recipe also comes in variations but I tried to find the most traditional one to include. For Generations of Creole home cooks, bread sone stale has been a fine excuse to make a warm and custardy bread puddings. The city's traditional French bread is the usual ingredient, since it is ideally light and readily soaks up the liquid ingredients, in addition to having a very thin crust, which means the crust need not be removed before it goes into the custard mix.

For 10 to 12 servings

A note: If New Orleans-style French bread is not available, you can get similar results using a sugarless, natural-yeast white bread with a low gluten content and a thin crust.

• The pudding can also be made with brioche, challah, day-old croissants or other egg bread, as long as the crust is very thin.

This recipe is prepared in two steps, requiring refrigerating the pudding for six or more hours before it is baked. The whisky sauce recipe will follow.

Ingredients

10 large eggs

2 3/4 cups whole milk

2 3/4 cups heavy cream

1 cup sugar, divided

1 1/2 teaspoons ground cinnamon, divided

1/2 teaspoon freshly ground nutmeg

1 piece day-old New Orleans-style French bread, about 23 inches long and weighing about 7 1/2 to 8 ounces

3/4 cup dark raisins

2 1/2 tablespoons unsalted butter, cut into small bits

Directions

1. In a large mixing bowl, lightly beat the eggs with a metal whisk or an electric mixer. Add the milk, cream, 3/4 cup of sugar, 3/4 teaspoon of cinnamon and the nutmeg.

2. Continue beating until the custard mixture is smooth and the sugar has dissolved. Set aside.

3. Cut the bread loaf crosswise into 1-inch slices.

4. Line the bottom of a 9-by-13-inch glass baking dish with the slices, cut sides up, squee2ing the slices in as necessary to form a single layer.

5. Pour the custard mixture over the bread and turn the slices over to assure they

are saturated. Scatter the raisins evenly over the bread, pushing them into the bread with your fingertips.

6. Cover and refrigerate for six to eight hours, preferably overnight.

7. Three to four hours before serving time remove the pudding from the refrigerator and allow it to reach cool room temperature, about one and a half hours.

8. Meanwhile, mix together the remaining 1/4 cup of sugar and 3/4 teaspoon of cinnamon, blending them well. Evenly dot the top of the pudding with the bits of butter and sprinkle the cinnamon sugar over the top.

9. Once the pudding has almost reached cool room temperature, preheat the oven to 325°F.

10. Place the pudding dish in a larger pan and carefully pour enough boiling-hot water into the outer pan to come halfway up the sides of the pudding dish. Cover both the baking dish and the outer pan with a single sheet of heavy-duty aluminum foil and seal the edges.

11. Bake the pudding until it is almost firm in the center, about one hour, then remove the foil and continue baking until the pudding is firm in the center and nicely browned, about 45 minutes more.

12. Remove the pudding and its water bath from the oven. Take the pudding dish out of the larger pan of water and let the pudding sit for 15 minutes at room temperature.

Serving Suggestion: Serve on heated dessert plates with some of the whiskey sauce spooned on each serving. Refrigerate any leftover pudding and sauce.

Whiskey Sauce: This recipe produces a sauce with a distinctive whiskey flavor. Served warm, it's perhaps the favorite embellishment for a Creole-style bread pudding. It also pairs well with ice cream or cake. When chilled, it is delicious with fresh berries.

For a scant 2 cups

Note: Reheating is not recommended, since this usually produces a texture similar to scrambled eggs

Ingredients

6 yolks from large eggs

1/2 cup sugar

1 cup heavy cream

1 teaspoon vanilla extract

1/4 cup Irish whiskey

Directions

1. In a large mixing bowl vigorously whisk together the egg yolks and sugar until light textured and a pale lemon color, about three minutes.

2. In a heavy 1-quart saucepan, bring the cream to a boil over medium-high heat, whisking constantly. Remove from heat and very gradually pour the cream into the egg mixture, whisking vigorously all the while.

3. Transfer the mixture to the top of a double boiler and place it over slow-simmering water.

4. Cook the sauce, whisking constantly, until it is noticeably thicker and coats the back of a wooden spoon, about eight minutes. Be careful not to overheat the sauce or let it boil. If lumps begin forming in it, remove it from the heat immediately and

whisk it until smooth before proceeding to finish cooking.

5. Remove from the heat and add the vanilla and whiskey.

Serving Suggestion: The sauce may be served immediately or kept in a warm spot until ready to serve.

Refrigerate leftovers to serve cold over fresh berries or the dessert of your choice.

EGGS

Most Cajun and Creole breakfasts include some kind of Egg recipes. I could not resist starting off with Maw-Maw's poached quail eggs. You can not get more traditional Cajun than this one.

Maw Maws Poached Quail Eggs

Stew 1 can of diced tomatoes and one green pepper shredded until reduced by half. Pour into hot platter and arrange toast on top. On each piece of toast place 2 poached quail eggs. Pour a small amount of melted butter, salt and pepper over eggs.

Eggs Sardu- A traditional New Orleans Poached Egg

Prepare the creamed spinach ahead of time. Use fresh or frozen artichoke bottoms (fresh is always preferable), but make sure they're the best quality. Warm them up and set the pan in a 175F oven; do the same with the creamed spinach. Prepare the hollandaise sauce and set the container in warm water while you poach the eggs. Assemble on warmed plates.

Ingredients

3 cups creamed spinach (recipe below)

6 large (or 12 small) artichoke bottoms

12 poached eggs

3 cups Hollandaise sauce

Creamed spinach

2 cups fresh spinach, cooked, well-drained and finely chopped

1 cup New Orleans-style Bechamel sauce (recipe below)

1/2 teaspoon freshly ground black pepper

1/4 teaspoon salt

Add the chopped spinach to the bechamel sauce and warm for a few minutes over low heat, stirring constantly. Mix in the salt and pepper, then set the pan in a 175F oven to keep warm until final assembly.

Bechamel Sauce New Orleans Style

Ingredients

2 tablespoons butter

1-1/2 tablespoons flour

3/4 cup milk

4 drops Tabasco

1/2 teaspoon salt

1 bay leaf

In a heavy saucepan melt the butter over low heat; do not brown. Add the flour gradually, stirring constantly to keep the mixture smooth. Do not allow the flour to cook. Once all the flour is blended in, gradually pour in the milk, stirring constantly with a wire whisk to keep the sauce perfectly smooth. Move the whisk around in the pan as your stir to blend the sauce at the bottom and sides. Once all the milk has been added, add the bayleaf and cook over low heat until the sauce thickens, then remove from heat and stir in the Tabasco and salt. Blend thoroughly.

Poaching the eggs

Break each egg you want to poach into an individual small cup. In a saute pan bring about 1-1/2 inches of water with 1 teaspoon of vinegar to a simmer. With the water simmering, slice each egg into the water from the cup by lowering the cup almost to the surface of the water and tipping it. Cook each egg for about 2 to 2-1/2 minutes in the simmering water, spooning some of the water over the surface of the egg during cooking. When the egg is cooked, lift out of the water with a mesh or slotted spoon, letting water drain off for a few seconds.

Poaching the eggs

Break each egg you want to poach into an individual small cup. In a saute pan bring about 1-1/2 inches of water with 1 teaspoon of vinegar to a simmer. With the water simmering, slice each egg into the water from the cup by lowering the cup almost to the surface of the water and tipping it. Cook each egg for about 2 to 2-1/2 minutes in the simmering water, spooning some of the water over the surface of the egg during cooking. When the egg is cooked, lift out of the water with a mesh or slotted spoon, letting water drain off for a few seconds.

Final assembly of the Eggs Sardou

Put 1/2 cup warm creamed spinach on each warmed plate. Place 1 or 2 warm artichoke bottoms on the bed of spinach, then set 2 poached eggs on the artichoke bottoms. Cover each portion with 1/2 cup hollandaise sauce. Serves 6.

COUCHE COUCHE/COUCH COUCH

(pronounced coosh coosh)

An old time traditional breakfast. Both Cajun and Creole people eat this. The creoles call it Couche Couche the Arcadians Couch Couch. Both serve it as a cereal with milk and sugar, honey or Molasses.

Couche Couche 1

Ingredients

1/4 cup oil

2 cups yellow cornmeal

1-1/2 teaspoons salt

1 teaspoon baking powder

3/4 cup milk

3/4 cup water

Heat the oil in a heavy pot or preferable a cast iron dutch oven.

Mix the dry ingredients, then add the milk and water. Pour the batter into the hot oil, and allow a crust to form on the bottom before stirring. Reduce heat to low and stir occasionally; cook for about 15 minutes.

Serve in bowls with milk and sugar, like a hot cereal.

Serves 4.

Couche Couche 2 (this one is very traditional using Lard/pig fat)

Ingredients

2 cups Cornmeal (preferably yellow)

1 1/2 teaspoon Salt

1 teaspoon Baking powder

1 1/2 cup Milk or water

1/4 cup Lard, melted and heated hot

Use a heavy iron pot or skillet. Mix the cornmeal, salt, baking powder and milk thoroughly and put into the heated shortening. Let a crust form. Give a good stir and lower the heat to simmer. Cover and cook for 15 minutes, stirring occasionally. Serves 6

Couch Couch 3(this one calls for shortening, today shortening is available in vegetable varieties)

Ingredients

2 Cups cornmeal

1-1/2 teaspoons salt

1 teaspoon baking powder

1-1/2 Cup milk

1/2 Cup shortening

Mix cornmeal, salt, baking powder and milk, mix thoroughly. Add the shortening. Place all the mixture into a hot skillet on high heat. Let a crust form. Stir, turn heat to low heat. Cover and cook for about 18 minutes.

GRITS AND GRILLADES

(pronounced "gree-ahds")

Grillades comes from the french word "to grill". This recipe was first created by the butchers in early Louisiana as the prepared a freshly killed pig for ham, sausage and other cuts of meat. Tiny cuts of meat called "grillades" were cooked in black iron skillets over coals of a wood fire.

Both Cajun and Creole cooks would save small trimmings of meat that they would accumulate from their daily meals and if they had accumulated enough they would make this dish for a brunch. Veal was the traditional meat of choice for this dish although round steak was also used. This dish is usually served with grits.

Creole Grillades and Grits

Ingredients

8 thinly pounded veal escallopes (scallops), about 3 ounces each

1/2 cup (1 stick) butter

1/2 cup olive oil

1/2 cup onion, finely chopped

1/2 cup green onions, finely chopped

3 cloves garlic, minced

1-1/2 cups bell pepper, finely chopped

1/2 cup celery, finely chopped

1 bay leaf

1-1/2 teaspoons Italian seasoning blend

4 ripe tomatoes, diced

1 tablespoon Worcestershire sauce

2 tablespoons tomato paste

1 quart beef stock (from scratch or a good canned brand)

2 tablespoons cornstarch

1/4 cup cool water

2 tablespoons fresh parsley, chopped

Salt and freshly ground black pepper to taste

Cooked grits

Season veal escallopes on each side with salt and pepper. Heat butter in a large skillet and sauté the veal until it is lightly browned, about 3 minutes per side. Transfer cooked meat to a platter and hold in a warm oven while prepping the sauce.

Heat olive oil in a large saucepan. Sauté the onion, green onion, bell pepper, garlic and celery until tender. Stir in bayleaf and Italian seasoning, and add the tomatoes, tomato paste and Worcestershire sauce.

When the mixture is well-blended, stir in the stock and cook for 5 minutes, stirring frequently. Make a slurry with the cornstarch and water, and stir it into the sauce to thicken it. Add the parsley. Season with salt and pepper to taste, and cook over medium heat until reduced by 1/4. Remove the bay leaf.

Spoon the sauce onto warm plates, and center a veal escallop on each. Place grits on the side of the meat, ladle additional sauce over the grits and meat. Garnish with parsley and a few capers. Serves 8

Cajun Grits and Grillades (Cajun Brunch In A Pot)

Ingredients

3 pounds beef round, sliced 1/4-inch thick, and cut into bite-size pieces

3/4 tablespoon salt

1/2 teaspoon cayenne pepper

1/2 teaspoon ground black pepper

1/4 cup flour

2-3 tablespoons bacon drippings

3/4 cup vegetable oil

3/4 cup flour

2 cups onions, minced

1 bell pepper, minced

3 cloves garlic, crush and chopped

3 whole tomatoes, with skins peeled, and minced

1/2 teaspoon thyme

1 bay leaf

1 tablespoon Worcestershire sauce

2 cups unsalted chicken broth

3/4 cup parsley

1 recipe from packaged grits

Salt and pepper the beef round, then dredge it in flour. Heat the bacon drippings in a Dutch oven, then brown the meat on all sides over high heat. Remove meat from pan and set aside

Now add the vegetable oil and flour, stirring the mixture over low heat to the point of almost burning (but not burning). You want a deep chocolate-colored roux. This could take up to 15 minutes, so be patient.

Toss in the minced onions and bell peppers, and garlic, and continue to stir until the onions turn completely brown (again, without burning), and the moisture is gone. Now add the tomatoes and stir them until the moisture in them is completely absorbed. The tomatoes will give a rosy hue to the roux.

Add the thyme, bay leaf, Worcestershire sauce, and chicken broth. Stir until well blended. Taste the mixture, and add salt, cayenne pepper, and/or black pepper to taste. If you like food spicy, this is where you can make it happen. Return the meat back into the roux, stir well, cover, and let cook slowly for about 1 1/2 hours. Stir occasionally. The sauce may thin out some as the meat renders liquid. You want the grillades to be so thick that a spoon laid on top will not sink, so keep cooking until you reach the right thickness. Also, you can remove the lid for the last 15 minutes of cooking to help thicken the pot.

When you are ready to serve, remove the bay leaf, and add the parsley. Serve the grillades over grits for the authentic Cajun brunch. It can also be served over rice.

Grillades is just as good, if not better, the second day. It freezes well too

Chapter 5: Mardi Gras Eats

Mardi Gras is a elaborate series of outdoor pageants and indoor balls that are held annually in the winter in Louisiana. The carnival culminates on Fat or Shrove Tuesday which is the day before Ash Wednesday and the beginning of Lent. It's the last hurrah of the catholic season so to speak.

Mardi Gras marks the Season between Christmas and Lent. Lent is a Catholic rite that lasts 46 days in which Catholics abstain from eating meat and other things considered vice for 46 days. Or, giving meat up for each friday in the 46 days of Lent. Devout Catholics will give up things like drinking and partying for that period too. So Fat Tuesday is the last day for those who observe Lent to party before their 6 weeks of abstinence. The residents of New Orleans and Louisiana are famous for their Mardi Gras Carnival times and party hardy as a result.

All Across Louisiana during Mardi Gras Time celebrations are occurring in each region. Keep in mind the food in Cajun country is rustic down home and the food in the City of New Orleans and where Creole people are is considered more citified and elegant. So there are certain dishes that are associated with Mardi Gras season. I tried to compile the most popular ones.

To Start all Creole and Cajun food have a mixture of spices that they use to season their foods with. Here are the recipes for a Basic Cajun and a Basic Creole Spice Mix. File powder is also a must. The spice mixes can be prepared ahead and stored in a jar to use when needed.

Basic Cajun Spice Mix

This spice mix can be prepared ahead and stored in a dry jar.

Ingredients

1/3 cup kosher salt

1/4 cup chili powder

1/4 cup Hungarian paprika

1 Tablespoon onion powder

1 Tablespoon coarsely ground black pepper

1 Tablespoon dried basil

1 Tablespoon dried oregano

1 Tablespoon ground coriander

1/2 teaspoon cayenne pepper

2 teaspoons dried thyme

1/4 teaspoon cumin

1/4 teaspoon white pepper

Combine all the above ingredients mix well store in a dry cool place tightly covered.

Creole Seasoning Mix

Here is a "Creole seasoning mix". Its prepared and stored like a Cajun Mix.

Ingredients

3 Tablespoons paprika

2 Tablespoons kosher salt

2 Tablespoons garlic powder

1 Tablespoon black pepper

1 Tablespoon onion powder

1-1/2 Tablespoons cayenne powder

1 Tablespoon oregano

1 Tablespoon thyme

File Powder (pronounced Fee Lay)- Which is ground sassafras basically. Filé powder (sometimes spelled "file powder" or called "gumbo filé") is made from dried and ground sassafras leaf. It is used as a seasoning and primarily thickening agent in gumbo, and has a wonderfully pungent and aromatic flavor. Common local brands are Zatarain's, Rex or Yogi. There is no substitute.

GUMBOS

Gumbo's are stew or soup that originated in Louisiana.   It is popular along the Gulf Coast of the United States and throughout the South.

Regardless of the region in Louisiana; Gumbo consists of a strong stock base of either meat, fish or shell fish, a thickener, the holy trinity and originally "okingumbo" or okra to which the word "Gumbo" derives from. Some ethnologists attribute the word   okingumbo to the Bantu who arrived as slaves from the word

ki ngombo meaning okra. Others attribute it to the Caribbean Spanish who pronounced Ki ngombo   guingambó or "qimbombó." And there are those who attribute the word gumbo to the Choctaw Indians who had the word kombo which means sassafras which is used in Gumbo.

A typical gumbo consists of a shell fish, poultry and a meat from pork shoulder. The poultry is usually either chicken, duck or quail. Local freshwater shell fish such as crawfish, crab or shrimp are used. Tasso or Andouille adds the smoky flavor to the dish.

There are several distinctions between the basic Cajun and Creole Gumbos. Creole Gumbo is medium light in color with tomato added. Traditional Cajun is darker and never uses tomatoes.   Another distinction is the use of okra as a thickener in Creole Gumbo and those recipes using file powder only add it after it is done. When okra is not in season file powder may be also used as a thickening agent.

CAJUN GUMBO SOUP

Ingredients

1 cup flour

1/2 cup oil

1 lg. onion

1 bunch green onions

2 stalks celery

1/2 bell pepper

1/2 cup parsley

1 dozen crabs

2 lbs. shrimp

2 lbs. smoked sausage

3 or 4 lbs. chicken, cut in pieces

2 tbsp. Cajun Herbed spice

1 tsp. Cajun Blend spice

1 dozen oysters

1/4 tsp. gumbo file, optional

Directions: First you make a roux; Brown flour in oil; add onions, celery, bell peppers. Saute until onions look brown, not burned.

Add chicken and sausage. Boil about 2 hours or until meat is cooked. Add cleaned crabs and shrimp. Cook another half hour.

Add seasonings, salt Cajun Blended and Cajun Herbed spices, red pepper and parsley.

Add oysters and cook for 5 minutes.

Add 1/4 teaspoon gumbo file, if desired.

CREOLE GUMBO   1 /Shrimp, Okra and Tomato Gumbo

Ingredients

2 pounds okra

1/4 cup vegetable oil

2 cups chopped, peeled and seeded fresh tomatoes or 2 cups chopped canned tomatoes

1 cup chopped yellow onions

1 cup chopped celery

1 3/4 teaspoon salt

1/2 teaspoon cayenne

5 bay leaves

1/2 teaspoon dried thyme

2 quarts shrimp stock or water

2 pounds medium shrimp, peeled and deveined

Chopped parsley and thinly sliced green onion tops for garnish

Wash the okra in cool water. Remove the caps and tips and cut into 1/4-inch rounds. Heat the oil in a large pot over medium-high heat. Fry the okra, stirring constantly, for 10 to 12 minutes, or until most of the slime disappears.

Add the tomatoes, onions, and celery and cook, stirring often, for 18 to 20 minutes, or until the okra and other vegetables are soft and the slime has completely disappeared.

Add the salt, cayenne, bay leaves, thyme and water. Stir and bring to a boil. Reduce the heat to medium and simmer, uncovered, for 15 minutes.

Add the shrimp and cook, stirring occasionally, for 30 minutes.

Remove the bay leaves and serve in deep bowls.

CREOLE SAUSAGE GUMBO 2

Makes 4 to 6 servings

Ingredients:

3 tablespoons olive oil

3 tablespoons all-purpose flour

1 (16-ounce) can stewed diced tomatoes

2 tablespoons ketchup

1 small onion, finely diced

1 chopped red bell pepper

1 tablespoon cilantro flakes

1 clove garlic, crushed

1-1/2 cups hot water

1 teaspoon salt

1/4 teaspoon fresh ground black pepper

1/4 teaspoon cayenne pepper

1/2 pound andouille sausage

Directions:

Heat oil in a deep skillet until hot. Add flour and stir well, cook until golden. Stir in tomatoes, ketchup, onion, bell pepper, cilantro, garlic, water, salt, black pepper and cayenne pepper. Bring mixture to a boil and then cook for 30 minutes at a simmer. . Add the sausage to the mixture and cook 10 to 15 minutes or until sausage is cooked through. Serve mixture over rice with hot sauce.

DIRTY RICE

Dirty Rice is traditionally from Cajun country stretching in out through Louisiana to Mississippi. Creole's have adopted this recipe. It's called "dirty rice" because its made from white rice with small pieces of chicken liver and giblets which give it a dark distinct flavor. It is used as either a rice dish or even stuffing. For those who are health conscious it can be made without the chicken liver and giblets. You can use ground pork and shredded baked chicken instead. Here are a couple of recipes for Cajun and Creole Dirty rice.

BAYOU DIRTY RICE

Ingredients

6 slices bacon -- diced

8 ounces ground pork

3/4 cup chopped onion

1/2 cup chopped celery

1/2 cup chopped green bell pepper

1/2 cup chopped red bell pepper

1 tablespoon minced garlic

1 teaspoon cayenne pepper

1 teaspoon salt

1 teaspoon freshly ground black pepper

1 teaspoon ground cumin

1/2 teaspoon ground oregano

1 cup long-grain rice

2 cups chicken stock or broth

8 ounces chicken livers -- trimmed, rinsed, patted dry, and minced

2 tablespoons fresh chives - snipped

Directions:

Place a large heavy saucepan or Dutch oven over medium heat, and saute the bacon until slightly crisp, about 5 minutes. Remove the bacon from the pan and drain off all but 1 tablespoon of the fat.

Add the pork and saute, breaking it up into small pieces, until it has changed color. Using a slotted spoon, remove the pork from the pan and add it to the bacon.

Add the onion, celery, bell peppers, and garlic to the pan. Saute over low heat for 5 minutes. Then add the cayenne, salt, black pepper, cumin, and oregano. Stir, and cook an additional 3 minutes.

Stir in the rice and cook 5 minutes. Add the stock and the reserved bacon and pork. Bring to a boil; then reduce the heat, cover, and simmer for 10 minutes.

Stir in the chicken livers and cook, covered, 5 minutes. Serve immediately, garnished with the chives.

This recipe for Bayou Dirty Rice serves/makes 8

CAJUN DIRTY RICE (easy recipe)

Ingredients

1 pound lean ground beef

1 pound beef sausage

1 onion, finely diced

1 (8 ounce) package dirty rice mix

2 cups water

1 (10 ounce) can diced tomatoes with green chile peppers

2 (15 ounce) cans kidney beans, drained

salt and pepper to taste

Directions:

In a skillet over medium heat, brown the ground beef, sausage, and onion; drain. In a large pan, combine rice mix and 2 cups water. Add diced tomatoes and chilies. Stir in the kidney beans. Bring to a boil, then add meat mixture. Season with salt and pepper. Return to boil, reduce heat, and cover, stirring occasionally. Cook for 25 minutes, until rice is easily fluffed with a fork.

CAJUN DIRTY RICE (this recipe, like all dirty rice can be used as stuffing

also)

Ingredients

1 lb. ground pork

1 lb. ground beef

1 large bell pepper

1 medium onion

5-6 cloves garlic, peeled

1-2 fresh, cayenne peppers

1 tsp. salt

1 tsp. red pepper flakes

2 4-6oz cans mushroom steak sauce

3-4 cups cooked rice

Directions:

Pan fry the ground meat well until all of the meat is well done. Put bell pepper, onion and garlic into food processor and "nearly" liquify it, then add this to the meat.

The pepper/onion/garlic should sizzle as you stir it well into the the meat.

When the sizzling fades, add the mushroom steak sauce and a little water and allow the entire dressing mix to simmer for at least a half hour.

As Dirty Rice: Cooked rice can be added to this mixture and thoroughly stirred. The more rice you add, the drier and "whiter" the resulting dressing will be.

Adding the right amount of rice will result in a dress that is moist with the rice appearing very brown ("dirty").

As Cornbread Dressing:

Substitute crumbed cornbread for cooked rice.

Save some for later: Freeze the dressing mix, i.e., before adding rice/cornbread, separately. When needed, defrost the mix by heating it and add the rice or cornbread.

CREOLE DIRTY RICE 1

<u>Ingredients</u>

6 cups rice, cooked

1/2 lb chicken gizzards

1/2 lb chicken livers

1/2 cup butter

1 tsp garlic, minced

1 cup each, onions, celery, green bell peppers, diced

1/2 cup butter shopping list

1 cup chicken stock

1/2 cup sliced green onions

1/2 cup parsley, chopped

salt and black pepper to taste

Directions:

Poach livers and gizzards in lightly salted water for about 45 minutes or until gizzards are tender. Remove and cool, reserving liquid. Set aside

Chop gizzards into small pieces, removing any tough membrane . Set aside

In large cast iron or a heavy bottom pan, melt butter using medium-high heat, saute livers until golden brown on all sides. About 15 minutes. Remove and cool, then chop into small pieces. Set aside

In same pan, saute onions, celery and bell peppers and garlic until barely wilted.

Return chopped livers and gizzards to pan with veggies and add chicken stock and small amount of poaching liquid.

Bring to boil and reduce until you have about 1/4 cup liquid. You need at least 1/4 cup but could have slightly more.

Fold in rice and stir in green onions and parsley. Season with salt and pepper

Note: Some modern cooks add about a pound each of cooked ground beef and sausage to make this a main dish casserole.

Creole Dirty Rice 2

Ingredients

1 lb of chicken or turkey gizzards ground or chopped very fine

1/2 lb of ground beef (chuck is preferable)

6-8 chicken livers chopped fine

1 bunch of green onions

1 large white or yellow onion chopped fine

2 toes of garlic chopped fine

1 rib of celery minced

1 small bell pepper minced

2 cups of cooked rice (cooled)

2 T flour

1 T vegetable oil

Salt, black pepper and cayenne to taste

1/4 cup of chopped fresh parsley

Directions:

In a large heavy skillet brown all of the meat over high heat with the 1 tablespoon of oil

Remove from pan with a slotted spoon

Add 2 Tablespoons of flour to the pan and brown slightly

Add onions, celery, bell pepper and garlic cook until onions are transparent

Return browned meat to the vegetable mixture and add the green onions

Add up to 1/4 cup of water if necessary and cook for 40 minutes

Add rice, salt, pepper, cayenne and parsley cook and additional 3 minutes

Serve with duck, turkey, chicken, pork or just off the spoon.

CREOLE DIRTY RICE 3

Ingredients:

1 lb. chicken giblets

1 lb. bulk pork sausage (ground pork)

1 cup onion, chopped

1/2 cup bell pepper, chopped

1/2 cup celery, chopped

2 cloves garlic, chopped

1/2 cup green onion tops, chopped

1/2 cup fresh parsley, chopped

6 cups cooked rice

Salt and pepper to taste

Directions:

Boil the giblets in salted water until very tender. You can add a quartered onion, a garlic clove, a stalk of celery, a bell pepper, and salt and pepper to the boil water. This will add flavor to the giblets, but do not grind or use them in the dressing.

Remove the giblets from the water, allow them to cool and put them through a food grinder or finely chop. Catch and save the juice from the grinder to moisten the dressing if need be.

In a heavy, deep skillet start the pork sausage on low heat, and as soon as fat begins to cook out, add the measured onion, bell pepper, celery, and garlic. Continue cooking on low heat, stirring occasionally, until all vegetables are soft.

Spoon or pour off any grease that may accumulate in the skillet. Add a little of the saved grinder juice and simmer the ground/chopped giblets with the pork sausage for 5-8 minutes.

Pour the giblet/sausage mix into a large (6 qt) pot. Add the cooked rice, green onion tops, parsley, salt and pepper, and stir all together thoroughly, but lightly. Do not let parsley and green onion tops become scorched. If you prefer, you can add the saved juice to moisten the dressing.

This recipe will serve 10-12.

Some Tips for Dirty Rice to make easier

For those recipes where the rice is already cooked ahead: Cook and cool the rice in advance. Don't forget to add salt to the water the rice is cooked in. Use cold rice to keep the dressing/dirty rice from being too mushy. Day ahead cooked is better

Add chopped fresh oysters to the dirty rice for a special flavor, especially during the holidays. Be cautious storing food when using fresh oysters. It won't last as long sitting on the cabinet.

Finely chopped ham can be added to or substituted for the giblets. Be careful with the salt since the ham will be salty. Always taste while you're cooking so you can fine tune the food as you go.

JAMBALAYA

Jambalaya is originally a Creole influenced dish. It originated in the French Quarters in New Orleans in the original European Sector. It was the Spaniards attempt of making Paella in the New World. Tomatoes were substituted for saffron to give it the red color that traditionally turns Paella Reddish in color. For this reason Creole Jambalaya is also called "Red Jambalaya. Cajun Jambalaya does not use tomato and is brown in color.

As far as the origin of the word "Jambalaya" goes Jambon in french means ham, jamon in Spanish means ham, ya ya was the name the west african's used for rice thus the word Jam a la ya rose. Another theory to the word's origin is the spanish word Jamon and Paella combined.(figure that one out to mean jambalaya

  Anyway if one goes to the Louisiana countryside you won't find tomatoes and in some cases even the holy trinity in the Jambalaya. Cajun's call it Brown Jambalaya. They usually make their Jambalaya with chicken or pork, sausage and onions. In New Orleans Jambalaya always has some kind of sea food in it, the holy trinity and tomatoes. Hence it is called Red Jambalaya by Creole people. Red Jambalaya may many times replace chicken with shrimp or crawfish.

Here are recipes for both:

CAJUN BROWN JAMBALAYA 1

This one has the celery and onion but no bell pepper, seafood or tomatoes

Ingredients:

1 lb. smoked sausage, sliced

1 1/2 lb. boneless chicken, cut in small strips

1 bell pepper, chopped

2 ribs of celery, chopped

2 medium onions, chopped

1-3 tbs. chopped garlic

1 can of chicken stock

2 1/2 cups of rice

thyme, parsley

cayenne pepper, black pepper, salt

Directions:

Brown sausage in a large iron pot. When thoroughly browned, remove and add chicken. Allow chicken to stick to the bottom of the pot before stirring. Scrape bottom of the pot with a wooden spoon to loosen browned bits.

Remove chicken and add bell pepper, celery, and onion. Wait about 2-3 minutes before stirring. As the vegetables begin to sweat, scrape bottom of the pot with a wooden spoon to loosen browned bits.

Return chicken and sausage to pot, adding 5 cups of water and all remaining ingredients except rice. Cover and bring to boil.

Add rice and reduce heat to simmer. Cover for 20 minutes. Do not lift lid until time is up, then remove lid and stir.

If jambalaya is a little soupy, let it stand uncovered for a few minutes .(Note: It is important to brown the meats and vegetables fully. This is what gives the jambalaya its color and rich flavor.)Also pork, shrimp or crawfish can be substituted for the chicken and or sausage.

CREOLE   JAMBALAYA 1

Ingredients

1 lb. smoked ham (cubed)

1/2 lb. chaurice* (hot sausage cut in pieces)

1/2 lb. smoked sausage (cut in 1/2-inch slices)

1 cup chopped onions

3 cups uncooked rice

1/4 cup chopped green onions

1/2 tsp. paprika

1 tbsp. chopped parsley

1 tsp. ground thyme

1 tsp. chopped garlic

1/2 cup chopped green pepper

1 tsp. salt

1 bay leaf

1 lb. shrimp (peeled and deveined)

4 cups boiling water

Directions:

Place ham, sausages, and onions in 3-quart saucepan. Cover and cook over medium heat until onions are soft. No need to add any oil as the meat will provide enough fat for cooking.

Add rice and stir well. Add all other ingredients. Bring to a boil. Let boil for 5 minutes. Lower heat. Cover pot tightly and let cook slowly for 35 minutes or until rice is tender. With a fork, fluff rice up, mixing sausages well.

CREOLE JAMBALYA 2

Ingredients

1/4 pound butter

1 lb andouille sausage, sliced

1 lb ham, diced

11/2 cups onions, chopped

11/2 cups celery, chopped

1 cup red bell pepper, diced

11/2 tbsp garlic, chopped

3 cups Uncle Ben's rice, raw

2 cups cooked chicken, diced

5 cups chicken stock

1 8-ounce can tomato sauce

1 Creole tomato, diced

1 bay leaf

1/2 tsp thyme

1/4 tsp cumin

1 tbsp basil

salt and pepper to taste

2 lbs 50-count shrimp, peeled

1 cup sliced green onions

Directions:

In a large Dutch oven, melt butter over medium-high heat. Add andouille and ham and continue to cook until lightly caramelized on the bottom of the pot, 10-15 minutes.

Add onions, celery, bell pepper and garlic. Continue to sauté until vegetables are wilted, 3-5 minutes. Stir in rice and chicken, blending well into the vegetable mixture.

Add chicken stock, tomato sauce, tomatoes and spices. Bring mixture to a rolling boil, reduce to simmer and cook on low heat, covered, for 30 minutes. Take care that heat is low enough to prevent scorching.

Add shrimp and green onions, stirring well into the mixture, cover and cook 10 additional minutes or until shrimp are done. Serve as a main course or as a stuffing for chicken or seafood.

ETOUFEE

This is a word borrowed from the french that means smothered or suffocated. It's typically served with Seafood or Chicken. It means to smother, stew or braise in cooking terms. Sometimes sausage is added to the pot. It is similar to Gumbo. Etoufee is served as an entree always while Gumbo may be considered a soup. Both are served with rice and Gumbo can be a main dish also.

ETOUFEE LIKE MAW MAW USED TO MAKE CAJUN STYLE

Ingredients

1 cup butter

2 tablespoons all purpose flour

2 onions minced

1 green bell pepper diced

3 cloves garlic diced

16 ounces cleans crawfish tails

1 teaspoon ground cumin

1/8 tablespoon Worcestershire sauce

1/8 tablespoon hot sauce

Salt and pepper to taste

Directions:

In a stock pot, melt butter over medium heat. When butter is bubbling, add flour to make a roux, stirring constantly to prevent or remove any lumps. Cook the roux for 5 minutes. Do not brown.

Stir in onions and bell peppers; saute 10 minutes, or until onions are translucent.

Add garlic, and saute for 3 minutes.

Stir in crawfish tails. Slowly pour in enough water to reach a little thicker than soup-like consistency. Season with cumin, Worcestershire sauce, hot sauce, and salt and pepper. Reduce heat, and simmer for 10 minutes.

CREOLE   STYLE ETOUFEE

Ingredients

1/2 cup roux *

1/2 cup finely chopped onion

1/2 cup finely chopped bell pepper

1 small can diced rotel tomatoes

2 cups water

3 lbs of cleaned crawfish meat

1 tsp. each salt, pepper, garlic powder

dash of cayenne

1 cup finely chopped green onion tops for garnish

Directions:

Make a roux by browning "slowly" in a small iron skillet ...1/4 cup oil and 1/4 cup flour until it is dark brown. Do not rush this. Add chopped white onions and bell pepper.

Next add Rotel tomatoes, water and seasoning. Stir very well over medium high heat. Cover and reduce to low and simmer for about 15 minutes.

Add crawfish tail meat.... and raise heat to a slow boil. Cook for about 5 to 10 minutes. Take off the heat , Cover and let set while you cook a pot of white rice.

(About 3 cups of raw rice, 6 cups water, salt, and butter)Serve over the 'cooked' white rice and garnish each bowl with green onion.

A TRADITIONAL CREOLE ETOUFEE WITHOUT TOMATOES

Ingredients

1 pound freshly cleaned shrimp (headed, peeled, and deveined)

5 teaspoons unsalted butter

1/4 cup all-purpose flour

2 cups shrimp stock

1 cup diced yellow onion

1/2 cup diced celery

1/2 cup diced green bell pepper

2 tablespoons minced garlic

2 tablespoons Worcestershire Sauce

2 tablespoons minced parsley

1 teaspoon dried thyme

Salt and Black Pepper to taste

2 tablespoons Creole Seasoning*

*Creole Seasoning Recipe

2 tablespoons paprika

2 tablespoons garlic salt

1 tablespoon garlic powder

2 tablespoons onion powder

1 tablespoons ground white pepper

2 tablespoons Cayenne Pepper

1 tablespoons dried Oregano

1 tablespoon dried thyme

1 tablespoon dried basil

Directions:

Season the cleaned shrimp with 1 tablespoon Creole Seasoning and refrigerate.

Melt the butter in a large cast iron skillet; add onion, celery, and bell pepper. Sauté until the onions become translucent.

Whisk in the flour to start the roux. The color of the roux at this stage should be a blond color. Whisk constantly for 3-5 minutes. Stir in the rest of the Creole Seasoning. Gradually add the shrimp stock to the roux, whisking continuously. The roux should now have a paste-like consistency and be darker in color. Bring to a boil, then lower the heat and reduce to a simmer.

Add the garlic, thyme, Worcestershire sauce, salt, and pepper and let simmer for 20 - 30 minutes, stirring occasionally. The roux should become a dark-brown/ brick color.

Add the parsley and seasoned shrimp. Continue to cook for another 10 minutes or until the shrimp are cooked through. Serve over plain rice and enjoy

What Else Can You Add?

Yellow and red bell peppers can be added to the Etoufee alongside the green bell peppers to add vibrant color without changing the taste.

Hot sauce and jalapenos can be added for added spiciness.

Sausage, like the traditional Cajun Andouille sausage, blends nicely into the recipe.

Shrimp Stock Recipe

The Shells and tails from 2 lb. of Shrimp

1/2 Cup chopped Onion

1/4 Cup chopped Celery

2 Garlic Cloves

1 Lemon sliced

2 Fresh Bay Leaves

3 Sprigs Fresh Thyme

1 tsp. Black Peppercorns

Add all ingredients to a 2 qt. saucepan. Cover this with cold water, it should be about 6-8 Cups Cups. You'll need 1 1/2 Cups for the Etoufee. Bring almost to a boil, reduce the heat to a low simmer. Simmer for about 45 minutes to an hour. Strain.

Tip: When adding fresh Thyme to a simmered dish like this, I always bundle the Thyme tightly with butchers twine. The leaves will remove themselves while cooking, and you will get all of the flavor from the stems. When ready to serve just remove the bundle of stems along with your bay leaves.

SHRIMP ETOUFEE (this one has tomatoes)

Ingredients

2 Tbsp Creole Seasoning

4 Tbsp Unsalted Butter

1/2 Cup Onion, Finely Chopped

1/4 Cup Celery, Finely Chopped

1/4 Cup Bell Pepper, Finely Chopped

1/4 Cup Flour

3/4 Cup fresh Tomatoes, diced

1 1/2 Cups Shrimp Stock

2 Tbsp Minced Garlic

I bundle of Fresh Thyme

2 tsp Homemade Worcestershire Sauce

1 tsp Hot Sauce (I like Crystal or Louisiana Gold)

1/2 Cup Green Onions, thinly sliced

3 Tbsp minced Italian Parsley

2 lb Good Quality Shrimp, Peeled and Deveined, Save shells for the stock

3 Tbsp Unsalted Butter

Salt & Freshly Ground Black Pepper to taste

1 Recipe Creole Boiled Rice

Directions:

Season the shrimp with 1 Tbsp of the Creole Seasoning.

Melt the butter in a large cast iron skillet, add the onions, bell pepper, and celery, sauté until translucent.

Whisk in the flour to make a blonde roux, stirring constantly, about 3-5 minutes. Stir in the remaining Creole Seasoning. Add a small amount of the shrimp stock, stir well to form a paste, add the remaining stock gradually, whisking constantly. Bring to a boil, then reduce to a simmer. You may need a little more stock, but the end result should be the consistency of a gravy, not too thick, not too thin.

Add the tomatoes, garlic, Thyme, Worcestershire, and hot sauce, a little salt, black pepper, and Cayenne. Simmer for 20-30 minutes.

Add the shrimp, green onions, and parsley, simmer for 10 minutes more or until the shrimp are cooked through. Stir in the 3 Tbsp butter, and adjust the seasonings to taste.

Creole Boiled Rice

1 quart of Boiling Water

1 Cup Basmati or Jasmine Rice

2 Fresh Bay Leaves (If you have to use dried, do so, but damn..... the fresh are so

much better!)

1 Tablespoon Kosher Salt

1 Tablespoon Unsalted Butter (Optional)

1 quart of Boiling water / 1 cup of Rice

The goal here is not to absorb all of the liquid into the rice like most recipes. The goal is to make the rice tender, then drain the rice. Think Pasta.

Bring the water to a boil with the Bay leaves. Add the salt. Add the rice, stir to make sure the rice doesn't stick! Do Not Stir again! If you agitate the rice too much, it gets sticky! So give it a good stir, when it comes back to a boil, partially cover it. Cook for about 11 minutes, but taste it, don't trust me! It should have some bite, but a crunch is bad, Call it Al Dente, like I said, think Pasta. When it's tender, drain it, pluck out the bay leaves, and if desired, place it into a 400 degree oven with the butter patted on top for about 15 minutes; this helps dry the rice out.

Homemade Worcestershire Sauce

Ingredients

2 Tbsp Olive Oil

3 Medium Onions, Chopped

5 Serrano or Jalapeno Chilies, Chopped

10 Garlic Cloves, Chopped

1 Tbsp Black Peppercorns

2 oz. Anchovy Fillets

4 Cups Water

2 Quarts Distilled White Vinegar

2 Cups Steen's 100% Pure Cane Syrup

2 Cups Dark Corn Syrup

1 Cup Molasses

1 tsp. Whole Cloves

2 Tbsp Kosher Salt

2 Peeled and Chopped Lemons

3 Tbsp Tamarind Paste*

1/2 lb Fresh Horseradish, Peeled & Grated

*Tamarind (or Tamarindo) is a pod fruit native to tropical Africa, the Caribbean and Asia; not so native to most grocery stores. It can be found jarred in paste form in Indian markets and fresh in one really great produce market. The paste is more convenient.

Directions:

Combine the Oil, Onions, Chilies, and Garlic in a Heavy Dutch Oven (preference Cast Iron), sauté until the Onions are slightly softened. Add the remaining ingredients, bring to a boil, then down to a simmer. Simmer, stirring occasionally, until the mixture coats the back of a spoon, about 3 hours. Strain. Refrigerate.

**If you like, put this in sterilized mason jars, screw on hot lids tightly, and place in a hot water bath, covering the jars by 1 inch. Boil for 15 minutes then remove and let cool. Check the seals, tighten the lids. Keep in a cool, dark place indefinitely. Refrigerate after opening.

MUFFULETTA'S AND   PO BOY'S

Sometimes you don't feel like taking the pots out and you just want a sandwich. These are the two national types for Louisiana and New Orleans. Some say they would have never made it to Lundi Gras (Monday Carnival before Fat Tuesday) if they didn't nurse their hangovers from a Muffuletta.

The Muffuletta came to Louisiana via the Italian Sicilian Immigrants. Its origins began in the Central Grocery in New Orleans French Quarters. The Central Grocery is a small old fashioned grocery store that was founded in 1906 and is still up running today. Salvatore Lupo a Sicilian immigrant started this establishment in 1906 and ran it until 1946. When he retired his son-in-law took over. Today it is run by a grandson and two cousins.

The muffuletta is a round type of sesame bread. Its similar to focaccia bread. A traditional muffuletta consists of one muffuletta loaf, split horizontally. The loaf is then covered with a marinated olive salad, then layers of capicola, salami, mortadella, emmentaler, and provolone. The sandwich is sometimes heated through to soften the provolone.

The size of the muffuletta is enough to feed more than one person, and many stores sell quarter or half-muffulettas.

The olive salad consists primarily of olives, along with celery, cauliflower and carrot. The ingredients are combined, seasonings are added, covered in olive oil and allowed to combine for at least 24 hours. Prepared olive salad for muffulettas can also be bought by the jar.

Here are a few basic Recipes:

MUFFULETTA

Ingredients

1 10" round loaf Italian bread with Sesame seeds

1 Recipe Olive Salad

1/4 lb Genoa Salami (Oldani is the best,)

1/4 lb Hot Capicola (you can use regular Ham.)

1/4 lb Mortadella (San Danielle brand is suggested)

1/4 lb Mozzarella

1/4 lb Provolone

Muffuletta Olive Salad

1 1/2 Cups Green Olives, Pitted

1/2 Cup Calamatta Olives (or Black) Pitted

1 Cup Gardiniera (Pickled Cauliflower, carrots, celery, Pepperoncini)

1 Tbsp. Capers

3 each Fresh Garlic cloves, thinly sliced

1/8 Cup Celery, thinly sliced

1 Tbsp. Italian Parsley, finely chopped

1 Tbsp. Fresh oregano (When I have it in my garden) or 2 tsp. dried

1 tsp. Crushed red pepper flakes

3 Tbsp. Red Wine Vinegar

1/4 Cup Pimientos (Roasted red peppers) Recipe follows

1 Tbsp. Green Onions, thinly sliced

Kosher Salt & Freshly Ground pepper To Taste (salt may not be necessary)

Directions:

Crush each olive on a cutting board with your hand. Combine all ingredients.

Cover with:

Extra Virgin Olive Oil about 1 - 1 1/2 Cups

Put into a bowl or jar, cover and let the flavors marry for about a week.

Assembly:

Cut the bread in half length wise.

Brush both sides with the oil from your 1 week old olive salad, go a little heavier on the bottom.

Layer half of the Oldani on the bottom half of bread. Then the Mortadella. Then the Mozzarella, then the Capicola, Provolone, and the remainder of Oldani. Top this with the olive salad. Put the lid on and press it down without smashing the bread. Quarter it. You've just created pure heaven.

This recipe serves 4.

HOT MUFFULETTA

Ingredients:

4 soft French rolls

Extra-virgin olive oil

3 dashes red wine vinegar

6 cloves garlic, chopped

3 teaspoons drained capers

3 large pinches dried oregano, crumbled

1/2 cup chopped or diced roasted red pepper

4 mild pickled peppers, such as Greek or Italian, sliced

1/2 red OR other mild onion, very thinly sliced

1/2 cup sliced pimiento-stuffed green olives

1 large tomato, thinly sliced

4 ounces dried salami, thinly sliced

4 ounces Westphalian ham, smoked turkey OR mortadella

8 ounces thinly sliced provolone cheese

Directions:

Open rolls and pull out a bit of their fluffy insides. Sprinkle each cut side with olive oil and vinegar, then with garlic, capers and oregano. On 1 side of each roll, layer red pepper, pickled peppers, onion, olives, tomato, salami, ham and finally cheese. Close up tightly and press together well to help seal.

Heat a heavy nonstick skillet over medium-high heat and lightly brush outside of each roll with olive oil. Place sandwiches in pan and weight down or place in a panini press. Cook until golden brown on one side, then turn and brown second side. Sandwiches are ready when they are crisply golden and cheese has oozed a bit and crisped in places.

Cut into halves and eat immediately.

This recipe serves 4.

Po BOYS

Po Boys are traditional submarine or heros from Louisiana. They consist of either fried sea food or meat on a baguette like french bread. A "dressed" po' boy has lettuce, tomato and mayonnaise; pickles and onion are optional. Non-seafood po' boys will also usually have Mustard, but the customer is expected to specify whether he or she wants "hot" or "regular"-the former being a coarse-grained Creole mustard (such as that produced by Zatarain's) and the latter being American yellow mustard. Mother's Restaurant, a popular lunch stop in New Orleans on Poydras St., uses shredded green cabbage rather than lettuce for its dressed sandwiches.

The Po Boy has several interesting stories of origin. There are countless stories as to the origin of the term po' boy. One theory claims that "po' boy" was coined in a New Orleans restaurant owned by Benny and Clovis Martin, who were former streetcar conductors. In 1929, during a four-month strike against the streetcar company, the Martins served their former colleagues free sandwiches. Martin's restaurant workers jokingly referred to the strikers as "poor boys", and soon the sandwiches themselves took on the name. In Louisiana dialect, this is naturally shortened to "po' boy."

In his book The Art of the Sandwich, Jay Harlow suggests that the name "po' boy" comes from the French pour boire or "peace offering,", This idea stems from when men would come home after a night on the town, bringing an Oyster Loaf home as a peace offering to their wives. An oyster loaf-a whole loaf of French Bread, split, hollowed out, and buttered, loaded with fried oysters and garnished with lemon juice and sliced pickles is still often referred to as a "Peace Maker."

One restaurant in Bay St. Louis, MS, Trapani's, insists that the name "po' boy" came from a sandwich shop in New Orleans. If one was new to a bar and bought a nickel beer, then he got a free sandwich thrown in. This was sometimes called a "poor boy's lunch", which came to mean just the sandwich itself.

Another version stems from the many sandwich carts in poor neighborhoods throughout the '20s and '30s. Many would offer hot beef or pork sandwiches, or for only a nickel you could get a po' boy sandwich which was the sandwich minus the meat, but with the bread soaked in the meat juices.

One Louisiana native, recalls another version where the name is said to reference the school lunch carried by "poor children" who could not afford sliced bread. As such, their lunch consisted of a sandwich made with a split loaf of French bread. Hence, a "poor boy's" sandwich.

it is the po' boy that has had the greatest day-to-day impact on the local diet in Louisiana, even in the era of modern fast food. Many people still have it at least once or twice a week-it is eaten for lunch more than any other single dish. Po' boys are made at home, sold pre-packaged in convenience stores, available at deli counters and make up a sizable percentage of the menu options at most neighborhood restaurants.

Po BOY 1

Ingredients

1 pint shucked oyster

1/4 cup flour

1/4 cup corn meal

1 tablespoon Blackening spices of your choice

vegetable oil for frying

1/4 cup mayonnaise

1 chipotle pepper, minced

1/4 cup butter

1/4 cup Tabasco sauce

1/2 cup shredded lettuce

4 (6" size) Hoagie buns, sliced

Directions:

Drain the oysters. Mix the flour, corn meal and spices in a bowl, adding salt and pepper to taste. Dredge the oysters in the flour mixture to coat well.

Meanwhile heat the vegetable oil to a depth of 1 inch in a large pan over medium high heat until it reaches 375 F. Fry the oysters until golden brown, remove and drain on paper towels.

Mix the mayonnaise and chipotle pepper until well combined. Heat the butter and Tabasco sauce until butter is melted and well combined with the hot sauce.

Spread some mayonnaise mixture on both halves of the buns and spread some lettuce on the bottom half of the buns. Pour the hot sauce mixture into a bowl large enough to hold the oysters and add the oysters, tossing them to coat with the sauce.

Divide the oysters equally amongst the buns and serve hot.

This recipe serves 4

FRIED SHRIMP Po BOY

Ingredients

1 10-12" long piece of New Orleans Style French Bread

4 Tbsp Mayonnaise

3 Tbsp Creole Mustard (Zatarain's makes a good widely available Creole Mustard.)

Pickle Slices

3/4 Cup Shredded Lettuce

Tomato Slices (Optional)

Fried Shrimp for Filling (Recipe below)

Slice the bread horizontally about 3/4 of the way through, leaving it hinged.

Spread the Mayonnaise on the inside of the bottom portion of the bread, spread the Creole Mustard on the inside of the Top portion. Layer you pickles and Tomatoes (if using) on the bottom portion of the French Loaf. Fill with the lettuce, then top with the Fried Shrimp.

FRIED SHRIMP RECIPE

2 1/2 Cups Vegetable Oil for Frying

1/2 Cup A.P. Flour

1/4 Cup Corn Flour (Masa Harina)

1/4 Cup Corn Meal

2 Tbsp Creole Seasoning, in all

1 Egg

2 Tbsp Water

1 Cup Peeled & Deveined Medium Shrimp (I use Louisiana Shrimp)

Heat the oil to 360 degrees in a 2 qt. saucepan.

Season the flour with 1 Tbsp Creole Seasoning in a bowl.

In another bowl, Mix the egg well with 2 Tbsp of water.

In another bowl, Mix the Corn flour and Corn Meal and the remaining 1 Tbsp Creole Seasoning.

Dredge the shrimp in the seasoned flour, then the egg wash, then the corn product mixture. Fry in batches in the 360 degree oil until just golden brown. Do not overcrowd the pan, and let the oil come back to temperature before frying another batch.

MUFFULETTA STYLE Po BOY

Ingredients

pkgs (10 oz size) French rolls

1/4 cup Mayonnaise

1 tablespoon salad olive juice PLUS"PLUS" means this ingredient in addition to the one on the next line, often with divided uses

1 teaspoon salad olive juice

4 slices (1 oz size) fully cooked ham

1/4 cup chopped salad olives PLUS"PLUS" means this ingredient in addition to the one on the next line, often with divided uses

2 tablespoons chopped salad olives

4 slices (1 oz size) salami

2 tablespoons Ripe olives; chopped

8 slices (1 oz size) Mozzarella cheese

Split French rolls; place cut-side up on baking sheet. Combine mayonnaise and olive juice; spread on each roll half. Place one slice ham on bottom half of each roll; top with 1-1/2 tablespoons salad olives.

Place one slice salami on top of olives. Place 2 slices Mozzarella cheese on each remaining roll half.

Set all roll halves under broiler until cheese is melted and bubbly. Place cheese halves on top of meat halves, and slice to serve.

This recipe serves 4

KINGS CAKE

No Mardi Gras goes by without a Kings Cake. This cake was brought to Louisiana originally by the French and Spanish settlers.

The King's Cake is a custom dating back to the twelfth century in France. In twelfth century France a similar cake was made to symbolize the coming of the Three Wise Men bearing gifts on the 12 days after Christmas. These 12 days were known as the feast of Epiphany, 12th Night or Kings Day.

Originally, the Kings Cake was made round to symbolize the route that was circular that the kings took to fool King Herod who was trying to follow the wise men to kill the Christ child.

The Kings Cake actually has a small doll representing the Christ Baby; or a coin, bean or pea hidden in it. All of the items represent the Christ Child. In 1871 the tradition of picking the Mardi Gras Queen was determined by who found the hidden prize in the cake. It is considered good luck to find the figure hidden in the cake and that person is the one to have the next king's cake party in return.

In 1872 the Rex Krewe (Kings Crew) Mardi Gras Organization chose the festivals symbolic colors to be used as the cakes colors. The colors are Purple for justice, Green for faith and Gold for power.

Here are a few Kings Cake Recipes, the first is a vintage recipe dating back to 1901.

TWELFTH NIGHT or KINGS CAKE (1901 version)

Ingredients:

8 cups of all-purpose flour, sifted

6 eggs

1 cup granulated sugar

1 pound butter or shortening

2 cups whole milk, scalded then cooled to lukewarm

1/2 ounce yeast (2 1/4-ounce packages, or about 4 1/2 tsp)

2 teaspoons salt

Candies to decorate

To make the cake take 6 cups sifted flour, and put it in a large mixing bowl. Make a hole in the center of the flour, and put in a half-ounce of yeast, dissolved in a little warm water. Add the 2 cups milk. Knead and mix the flour with one hand, while adding the milk with the other. In another bowl, combine remaining 2 cups flour with the salt; set aside. In another mixing bowl, beat eggs with butter and sugar until light. Add to dough, kneading lightly with your hands, and adding more eggs if the dough is a little stiff. Let the dough rise until doubled in bulk, then add the reserved flour and salt.

Knead the dough by turning it over on itself three times and set to rise again, covered with a cloth for about an hour. Take it up and work again lightly, and then form into a ring.

This is a large amount of dough, so it may be divided and baked in two or more King's Cakes. Pat gently and flatten a little. Have ready a greased parchment paper or silpat-lined baking pan, and set the ring in the middle. Cover the pan with a clean cloth, and set the cake to rise for an hour longer. When well risen, glaze the loaves lightly with a beaten egg. Place in 325° oven; let bake for 1 to 1 1/2 hours, or less if making smaller loaves. Decorate with colored icings and decorator candies, as desired.

EASY MARDI GRAS KINGS CAKE

This cake recipe is similar to making filled coffee cakes or Danish Pastries. You can substitute the cream cheese filling for pie filling if you wish.

Ingredients

Filling:

4 ounces (half of a large block) cream cheese

1/2 cup brown sugar, packed

1/2 teaspoon ground cinnamon

1/4 cup raisins, soaked in hot water for 15 minutes, drained, and patted dry on paper towels

1/2 cup pecan halves

Cake:

2 rolls (total of 12 individual crescent rolls) refrigerated crescent rolls in the can

Icing:

1-1/2 cups confectioners' sugar (powdered sugar)

3 to 4 Tablespoon (about) milk or cream

1 teaspoon pure vanilla extract

Purple, green, and yellow colored sugar crystals or food coloring

Directions:

Lace cream cheese, brown sugar, cinnamon, and raisins in the bowl of a food processor fitted with the metal blade. Process until combined. Add pecan halves and pulse until pecans are chopped to about 1/4-inch pieces. Set aside.

Preheat oven to 350 F. Spray a pizza pan or baking sheet with butter-flavored vegetable oil.

Unroll crescent roll dough and separate into triangles. Position triangles next to each other with the points toward the center, overlapping the long sides about 1/4-inch, forming a large round. Where the pieces overlap, press the seams together only in the center of each seam, leaving either ends of the seams unsealed so you can fold them up over the filling.

Spread the filling around in a ring covering the center sealed seam of each triangle.

Place a small plastic baby or dried bean somewhere in the filling. (The person who gets this piece will have good luck for the year.)

Fold the short side of each triangle toward the center just to the edge of the filling to cover. Then pull the point end of the triangles toward the outer rim of the pan to fully enclose the filling, tucking under the points. Lightly press the seams.

Bake 20 to 25 minutes until golden brown. Let cool to room temperature.

Whisk together the confectioners' sugar, milk or cream, and vanilla until smooth. The consistency should be fairly thick, but still thin enough to slowly drip down the sides. Add more milk as necessary. Spoon the icing in a ring over the top of the King Cake and allow it to slowly drip down the sides.

To decorate for Mardi Gras, sprinkle wide stripes of purple, green, and yellow colored sugar crystals.

If using food coloring, whisk together icing as above. Divide icing evenly amongst 3 bowls. Add 2 drops each of red and blue food coloring to the first bowl to make purple. Use 2 drops each of yellow and green in the remaining 2 bowls. Scrape each individual bowl into its own zip top bag. Squeeze out all the air and seal. Snip off one corner of the bag and use as a pastry bag to pipe wide stripes of icing on the King Cake. The bags will give you more control than using a spoon or spatula.

The icing should firm up a bit in about an hour.

Yield: 12 to 16 servings

Kings Cake 3

Ingredients

1/2 cup warm water (110 to 115 degrees)

2 packages active dry yeast

1/2 cup plus 1 teaspoon sugar

3 1/2 - 4 1/2 cups flour unsifted

1 teaspoon nutmeg

2 teaspoons salt

1 teaspoon lemon zest, this is lemon rind, grated

1/2 cup warm milk

5 egg yolks

1 stick butter cut into slices and softened, plus 2 tablespoons more softened butter

1 egg slightly beaten with 1 tablespoon milk

1 teaspoon cinnamon

1 1" plastic baby doll

Directions:

Pour the warm water into a small shallow bowl, and sprinkle yeast and 2 teaspoons sugar into it. Allow the yeast and sugar to rest for three minutes then mix thoroughly. Set bowl in a warm place for ten minutes, or until yeast bubbles up and mixture almost doubles in volume. Combine 3 1/2 cups of flour, remaining sugar, nutmeg and salt, and sift into a large mixing bowl. Stir in lemon zest. Separate center of mixture to form a hole and pour in yeast mixture and milk. Add egg yolks and, using a wooden spoon, slowly combine dry ingredients into the yeast/milk mixture. When mixture is smooth, beat in 8 tablespoons butter (1 tablespoon at a time) and continue to beat 2 minutes, or until dough can be formed into a medium-soft ball.

Place ball of dough on a lightly floured surface and knead like bread. While kneading, sprinkle up to 1 cup more of flour (1 tablespoon at a time) over the dough. When dough is no longer sticky, knead 10 minutes more until shiny and elastic.

Using a pastry brush, coat the inside of a large bowl evenly with one tablespoon softened butter. Place dough ball in the bowl and rotate until the entire surface is buttered. Cover bowl with a moderately thick kitchen towel and place in a draft-free spot for about 1 1/2 hours, or until the dough doubles in volume. Using a pastry brush, coat a large baking sheet with one tablespoon of butter and set aside.

Remove dough from bowl and place on lightly floured surface. Using your fist, punch dough down forcefully. Sprinkle cinnamon over the top, pat and shake dough into a cylinder. Twist dough to form a curled cylinder and loop cylinder onto the buttered baking sheet. Pinch the ends together to complete the circle. Cover dough with towel and set it in draft-free spot for 45 minutes, or until the circle of dough doubles in volume. Pre-heat oven to 375 degrees.

Colored sugars

Green, purple, & yellow paste

12 tablespoons sugar

Squeeze a dot of green paste in palm of hand. Sprinkle 2 tablespoons sugar over the paste and rub together quickly. Place this mixture on wax paper and wash hands to remove color. Repeat process for other 2 colors.

Icing

3 cups confectioners sugar

1/4 cup lemon juice

3 - 6 tablespoons water

Combine sugar, lemon juice and 3 tablespoons water until smooth. If icing is too stiff, add more water until spreadable. Spread icing over top of cake. Immediately sprinkle the colored sugars in individual rows consisting of about 2 rows of green, purple and yellow.

Louisiana Kings Cake

Here's a traditional New Orleans style King's cake recipe

Ingredients:

Brioche:

1/2 cup warm water, about 105 to 115 degrees

2 envelopes active dry yeast

4 1/2 to 5 1/2 cups sifted flour

1/2 cup sugar

1/2 teaspoon freshly grated nutmeg

2 teaspoons salt

1 teaspoon grated lemon zest

1/2 cup lukewarm milk

3 eggs

4 egg yolks

1/2 cup butter, softened

2 tablespoons butter

1 egg, lightly beaten

with 1 tablespoon milk

a tiny doll or coin

Icing:

3 cups confectioner's sugar

1/4 cup lemon juice, strained

3 to 5 tablespoons water

2 candied cherries, halved

Sugar Topping

Paste food coloring: purple, green, and yellow

3/4 cup sugar

Brioche:

Combine yeast and the warm water. Combine flour, sugar, nutmeg and salt in a large mixing bowl. Stir in lemon peel. Make a well in center and add yeast and water mixture, along with milk. Lightly beat the 3 eggs and 4 egg yolks; add to liquid mixture. With a large wooden spoon, gradually incorporate dry ingredients into liquids in the center well. Beat in 1/2 cup of the butter and continute beating until dough forms ball. Use a food processor or dough hook for beating, if desired. Place ball on floured board and knead until smooth and elastic, incorporating more flour as necessary, a little at a time. Butter the inside of a large bowl with 1 tablespoon of the butter. Place dough in bowl and turn so the entire surface will be buttered Cover bowl and set aside for 1 to 1 1/2 hours, or until doubled in bulk. Brush a large baking sheet with remaining butter. Punch dough down on lightly floured surface. Knead, then pat and shape dough into a cylinder about 14 inches long. Place on baking sheet and form into a ring. Press bean or doll well into dough so that it doesn't show. Set aside again to rise for about 45 to 60 minutes. When ready to bake, brush the top and sides of the ring with the egg-milk mixture. Bake the King's Cake in middle of oven at 375° for 25 to 30 minutes, or until golden brown. Slide cake onto wire rack to cool.

Icing:

Combine the confectioners' sugar, lemon juice and 3 tablespoons of water in a deep bowl; stir until the icing smooth. If too stiff to spread, beat in 1 teaspoon water at a time, until desired consistency is reached. It should be thin enough to run slowly down the sides of the cake. Spread the icing over the top of the cake, letting it to run down the sides. Prepare the colored sugars:

Squeeze a dab of green paste into the palm of one hand. Sprinkle 2 tablespoons of sugar over the paste and rub hands together to color the sugars evenly. Put colored sugar in a cup and repeat process with green, then twice with purple and yellow, putting each color in a separate cup.

Sprinkle the colored sugars over the icing immediately, forming a row of purple, yellow, and green strips, each about 2 inches wide, on both sides of the ring. Arrange cherry halves evenly on top of the cake, pressing them gently into the icing.

Beignets

The word Beignet actually has celtic origins from the word Bigne which means "to raise". It is also the french word for fritter. Beignets are fried pieces of raised yeast dough that after fried are sprinkled with sugar or iced. They are like sweet doughnuts with out a hole in the middle.

It was the French Colonists who brought the Beignet to Louisiana in the 18th Century. For years Beignets were ball shaped and covered with mocha frosting. Later it was cut and shaped into a doughnut hence the raised doughnut was born.

The Cafe de Monde located in New Orleans still stands and serves Beignets and Cafe au Lait since 1862. Cafe au Lait is Dark roasted Coffee with chicory and steamed milk. Chicory was added to the coffee originally to stretch the coffee but also was found to add a smoother richer taste to the brew.

Here are some Beignet recipes Bon mange

You can take the basic recipe and fill them with a custard or a sweet jam and then ice them if you wish.

Ingredients

1 1/2 c. warm water (110 degrees)

1 pkg. dry yeast

1/2 c. sugar

1 tsp. salt

2 eggs, room temp.

1 c. evaporated milk

7 c. flour

1/4 c. veg. oil

Oil for deep frying

Powdered sugar

optional to add to the batter:

1 tablespoon of cinnamon

1 teaspoon of cardamom

a sprinkle of nutmeg

*The only other advice would be to add 4 cups of flour initially and work that into the batter really well, then add 1/2 cups at a time. I ended up only using 6 cups of the flour to make the dough have the right consistency.

Fillings or toppings (the dough puffs up leaving a nice space inside

 to fill)

Directions:

In a large bowl, sprinkle yeast over water; stir until dissolved. Beat in sugar, salt, eggs and evaporated milk. Gradually beat in 4 cups flour and the oil. Add remaining flour gradually and beat until a smooth dough forms. Cover bowl and refrigerate overnight.

Roll dough on a floured board to 1/4" thick. Cut into rectangles 2 1/2" x 3 1/2". Heat oil in deep fryer to 360 degrees. Fry four rectangles at a time for 2 to 3 minutes. Drain on paper towels.

Keep beignets warm in a 200-degree oven until serving. Just before serving, sprinkle with powdered sugar

Step one proofing the yeast:

Step 2 Adding the additional or optional spices

Step 3 Adding Additional flour until you get the right consistency

After resting over night it is ready to roll out cut and fry:

Fry in the oil and...

Voila Beignets

You can use a pastry bag to fill the middles with custard or jam..and use powdered sugar or frost

Beignets 2 (this recipe has butter)

<u>Ingredients</u>

cup lukewarm water

1/4 cup sugar

1/2 teaspoon salt

1 egg, room temperature and beaten

2 tablespoons butter, softened

1/2 cup evaporated milk

4 cups bread flour or all-purpose flour

3 teaspoons instant active dry yeast

Vegetable oil*

Powdered sugar for dusting

* Use just enough vegetable oil to completely cover beignets while frying.

Using a mixer with a dough hook, place water, sugar, salt, egg, butter, evaporated milk, flour, and yeast in the bowl. Beat until smooth.

If using a bread machine, select dough setting and press Start. When dough cycle has finished, remove dough from pan and turn out onto a lightly oiled surface. form dough into an oval, place in a lightly greased bowl, cover with plastic wrap, and refrigerate until well chilled (3 to 4 hours) or overnight.

To prepare dough, remove from refrigerator and roll out on a lightly floured board to 1/2-inch thickness. Cut into approximately 3-inch squares or circles.

In a deep fryer or large pot, heat vegetable oil to 360 degrees F. Fry the beignets (2 or 3 at a time) 2 to 3 minutes or until they are puffed and golden brown on both sides, turning them in the oil with tongs once or twice to get them evenly brown; beignets will rise to the surface of the oil as soon as they begin to puff. NOTE: If the beignets don't rise to the top immediately when dropped into the oil, the oil is not hot enough. Remove from oil and drain on paper towels, then sprinkle heavily with powdered sugar. Serve hot.

The dough can be kept for up to a week in the refrigerator - it actually improves with age; just punch down when it rises. Dough can also be frozen; cut and roll, or shape doughnuts before freezing.)

Makes 18 beignets.

Cajun Beignets

Ingredients

1/2 cup shortening

2 packages yeast

1 tsp salt

2 eggs , well beaten

1/2 cup sugar

6 1/2 cup flour

1 cup evaporated milk

Take 1/4 cup warm water and mix in the yeast until it is all dissolved and set aside.

Cream shortening , sugar and salt together then add one cup boiling water and one cup milk to the mixture stirring in until well mixed then set aside. Now add your yeast and beaten eggs to the cream mixture making sure you mix well.

Now add 3 1/2 cups flour to that mixture beating well with a spoon, now add the remainder of the flour again mixing well. When done grease a container and set the dough in covering it and chill in the fridge.

Just before you roll out dough warm your deep fryer to 360 degrees . I use shortening.

When ready roll out dough into a square about a 1/4 inch thick and cut into three inch squares with a knife then cut a 1/2 inch slit in each square.

Then drop them in a few at a time until golden brown covering them in powdered sugar as they come out. You can drain them a bit on a paper towel then roll them in powdered sugar.

Creole style beignet batter (this is more like a fritter you drop batches of the batter in the hot oil)

Ingredients

1 cup flour

2 eggs, separated

2 tablespoons good brandy

1/2 teaspoon salt

cold water

1 tablespoon melted butter

fruit chunks

Beat the yolks of the eggs well and add the flour, beating very light. Add the melted butter and the brandy, and thin with a little cold water to the consistency of a very thick batter. Beat egg whites to thick peaks; add to the batter, and then dip the fruit into this, immersing well at one dipping. Heat oil to 360°. With a tablespoon, drop battered fruit into the hot oil and fry to a golden brown. The batter must be thick enough to coat the fruit all around in one immersion, yet it should not be so thick as to be over heavily coated or tough.

French Market Style Beignets

This version of Beignets can be made at the last minute because it does not require kneading or rising time. It is so easy that you'll find yourself whipping up a batch whenever you are in the mood for a little something sweet.

Ingredients

Oil for frying - safflower or other oil with a high smoke point

1-3/4 cups sifted flour, plus extra for rolling

1/2 teaspoon baking powder

1/8 teaspoon salt

2/3 cup sugar

2 large eggs

1/2 teaspoon pure vanilla

2 tablespoons canola or safflower oil

2 tablespoons milk

1/2 cup powdered sugar

Fill a heavy pot (or 2-1/2" deep cast iron skillet) halfway with oil. Be sure to use good frying oil with a high smoke point. Heat over a medium-high flame until oil reaches a temperature of 360 degrees F.

While the oil is heating up, lightly beat the eggs with a wire whisk in a large bowl. Stir in sugar and vanilla. Stir milk and oil (canola or safflower) into sugar-egg mixture. Add the flour, baking powder and salt into a sifter or sieve and sift directly into egg mixture. Stir until a biscuit-like dough forms.

Lightly flour a work surface and turn out the dough. If the dough is too sticky, gently work in a small amount of flour. The dough will be tough if overworked. Sprinkle dough lightly with flour and gently roll the dough out to a thickness of 1/8-inch. Use a sharp knife or pizza cutter to cut rolled dough into 2-inch squares. Resist the temptation to remix the scraps. They will be tough so just fry up the odd bits just as they are.

Use a dough scraper or spatula to gently lift the cutout dough off the work surface and into the hot oil. Fry the beignets, a few at a time, until golden, turning as necessary, with a slotted spoon. When both sides are golden, remove from hot oil and allow the beignets to drain on paper towels. Dust heavily with sifted powdered sugar and serve immediately.

Makes about 1 dozen Beignets

Chapter 6: Conclusion:

This is a drop in the bucket of the rich cuisine of the Cajun and Creole peoples who reside in the Louisiana Region of the United States. Depending on where you live some of the ingredients may be hard to get to make some of the recipes. Below is a wonderful cookbook that I recommend you should get loaded with best recipes from your favorite restaurant -- you can also do a Internet search about other kinds of Cajun and Creole cooking.

www.ingramcontent.com/pod-product-compliance
Lightning Source LLC
Chambersburg PA
CBHW081624100526
44590CB00021B/3590